Ready, Set, Speak
ESL Active Learning

by
Barbara Agor
Stewart Agor

Frank Schaffer Publications®

Authors: Barbara Agor, Stewart Agor
Development House: Words & Numbers
Design and Production: Ophelia M. Chambliss

Frank Schaffer Publications®

Send all inquiries to:
Frank Schaffer Publications
3195 Wilson Drive NW
Grand Rapids, Michigan 49534

Ready, Set, Speak: ESL Active Learning

ISBN: 0-7682-3072-1

2 3 4 5 6 7 8 9 10 PAT 10 09 08 07

Contents

Introduction

When we sat down to write this book, wondering where to start, a friend said, "Just look back over your decades of teaching and call up pictures." The first and most enduring picture that came to mind was one of Barbara's—a small sixth-grade class in an urban school. There were only a dozen students, but on some days, it felt like there were fifty little bodies in the small classroom. Three of the boys simply couldn't stay in their chairs. Teacher and students finally came to an agreement: If each boy had one hand touching his chair, that was good enough.

Though these students were English language learners—students who first spoke a language other than English—much of what they needed is equally valuable to classmates who have spent their entire lives speaking nothing but English. We hope that, as you read through the five chapters of this book, you will find much that works in a class of English language learners, a class of native speakers of English, or a mixed class containing both. We believe that you will, because many of the activities were co-invented and written by Stewart, who spent almost all his career teaching what we call "regular" English in a suburban school.

A BRIEF OVERVIEW OF *READY, SET, SPEAK*

As you wander through the five chapters that follow, dip in almost anywhere that interests you. Though much of the teaching and learning happens through commands, these are not scripts to follow word-for-word but rather examples of how a series of commands leads to a certain kind of learning.

The first chapter, "Simple Responding," is especially for those who have not yet tried teaching by pairing commands with movement and who want to try a few things quickly and easily. Chapter 2, "Visualizing Language," and Chapter 5, "Games, Word Play, Songs, and Chants," also offer quick get-your-feet-wet activities as well as some longer activities and variations.

After you have tried any one of the four Arenas in Chapter 3, you will never look upon your classroom in the same way again. The Arena is a space that you and your students create within your classroom. One day it is a living room, and another it's a bunch of sports channels on television. New Arenas will just keep inventing themselves.

Unlike the activities in other chapters, those in Chapter 4 should be applied in the order they are presented, from the opening pantomime through to the end of the chapter. Chapter 4 evolves through the repetition and transformation of one story, "Cinderella." It even includes a variation in which Cinderella is male—the brave Irish Billy Beg.

Underneath the Activities

Looking back over our decades of teaching at all levels from kindergarten to geriatric, we can see some of the reasons for the successes that we have had. And we can see even more clearly the reasons for our failures. We have distilled this experience into a few principles that underlie the chapters you are about to read.

1. Move students around. Movement doesn't simply support learning, movement is learning. Those three boys in Barbara's sixth-grade class were happiest when they were learning on their feet. The enormously complicated process of producing speech occurs more in the body than the brain through what sports people call muscle memory. Like learning to juggle, learning to speak a language involves physical practice and rehearsal as it advances from clumsiness to coordination.

2. Make your language understandable. Unless you have sat for hours upon hours in a classroom where you did not understand the language, it is difficult to imagine the stress and exhaustion that English language learners experience. Adults have told us that they can manage about twenty minutes of full concentration at a time. We suspect younger students can manage considerably less.

3. Be aware of how language learning takes place. As language teachers, we love linguistic analysis. The discovery and application of rules brings us exquisite joy. However, our way is not how most of the world learns languages, and it's unlikely to be the way most of your students do. Stephen Krashen, a noted English language learning expert, makes a useful distinction between learning, which he says is conscious and deliberate, and acquisition, which happens without our really knowing, sometimes almost in spite of ourselves.

    Some of this acquisition occurs during what has come to be known as the silent period. Persuasive research suggests that forcing speech too quickly actually harms language learning. So what do teachers offer students during this silent period? Opportunities to listen to understandable commands and to respond with their bodies—to be Ready and Set, as the title of this book suggests, before they Speak.

4. Be relevant, but not always. In these days of standards and account-

ability, we teachers feel great pressure to make sure that students have all the academic knowledge that they are supposed to and that they can demonstrate it at the right time and in the right testing formats.

However, a classroom does not always have to look like the end product—the test. Instead it can look like the end product that educators have traditionally prized—actively engaged students who can listen, think, talk, write, and learn. If we pay attention to the real goals of education, academic knowledge and good test scores will result.

5. Be outrageous. There's time enough later in life for our students to be serious. Take simple activities, like making a peanut butter sandwich, and produce an imaginary sandwich in which the fillings rest on a student's nose, with a slice of bread on each ear. Students can learn the same things by constructing a proper sandwich, but a human sandwich variation is much more fun. And if you can be outrageous, so can the students. The desire to be creative in their new language generates a need for more and more language.

In a similar vein, encourage imagination. In these days of television and computers, many students have had imagination served up to them rather than creating it by themselves. Chapter 3 of this book, "Acting in the Arena: The Imaginary Real World," will limber up their imaginations.

6. Teach under the radar. The art of teaching lies in being able to create situations that require specific knowledge but that don't necessarily start by explicit teaching of that knowledge. First comes the context and only after, the language.

For example, it's rarely effective to shriek every time that a student says "I seen." But you can call for a correction through a simple sawing motion—a silent teacher (see Chapter 2)—that the class has come to understand means I saw, not I seen. It's quick, it's painless, and it keeps the focus on meaning, rather than form.

We have enjoyed working on this book, and we hope it will spark many ideas for incorporating movement in your teaching. Special thanks to Louis Carrillo, Luz M. Aranda, Ophelia Chambliss, Martha Hansen, and especially to those well-remembered sixth graders—even the ones who could stay in their chairs.

Barbara Agor and Stewart Agor

Simple Responding

One of the most common and most effective ways to bring students' entire bodies into the learning process is to pair commands with simple student responses. The activities in this chapter apply that approach and set forth a range of learning possibilities.

As with most activities throughout the book, you can adjust the pace at which new words and expressions are introduced to assure student understanding. You can also assess that understanding by how well the students follow the commands.

While students will be conscious of learning the command verbs they hear as well as the objects and relationships that accompany those commands, some of these activities will also set the scene for future learning in ways the students may not realize at the time. When such components become part of the explicit curriculum later on, learning will become a process of recognition, of affirmation. You will hear "Oh, yeah!" rather than "Huh?"

This chapter sets forth the basic process of pairing commands with responses. As you apply the process, you will quickly see ways to extend and transform the activities. You will, for example, be able to use the techniques here to preteach the vocabulary required by other activities in subsequent chapters.

1.1 Survival Vocabulary

If you were to follow your students around for a day, you would collect a huge list of commands to which they must respond. A beginning English

---

language learner has no idea what most of these commands mean and has to rely on watching what others do—not a bad way of learning. Or they discover meaning by getting into trouble, as a result of ignoring commands that they do not understand.

EMERGENCIES

By their very nature, emergencies require quick response. Commands and physical response are associated with such crises, so actual or simulated emergencies provide realistic opportunities to understand and acquire language.

Basic fire drill behavior

No matter how carefully their teachers prepare students for the first fire drill of the year, they tend to be disasters, at least in my school. Upon hearing the alarm bell, it's not unusual for students to jump out of their seats, whirl around like chickens with their heads cut off, and then run toward the classroom door. Start by making a loud ringing sound.

 Sit down.
Be quiet.
Now, slowly stand up.
Walk slowly toward the door.
Make a line.
(to the first student) Open the door.
Be quiet.
Turn left.
Follow the other students.
(to subsequent students as they move through the door) Be quiet.
Follow the other students.
(You go through the door just before the last student, to whom you say) Close the door.

Who is the leader?

For many emergencies, particularly those in schools, it is possible to designate a leader. For fire drills, the group leader is usually a student who has already demonstrated responsibility and maturity. But another way of developing leadership (and, not incidentally, of learning language) is to affirm what most students understand—that the oldest student should take care of the younger ones. To determine who that student is, try creating an age line.

Before you start, find out all the years, months, and dates that your students will need.

➤ Raise your hand if you were born in 1992. (You write 1992 on the board, along with the number of students born in that year.)
Raise your hand if you were born in 1993. (Continue until you see that you have covered all the possible years.)
Raise your hand if you were born in January. (Write *January* on the board, along with the number of students with January birthdays. Continue throughout the year.)
(Make a list of all possible numbers, from first through thirty-first, probably written as 1st, 2nd, etc.)
Raise your hand if you were born on the first.
...on the second   Etc.

Put a stack of 3-x-5 cards on your desk.

➤ Come to my desk.
Take a card.
Write the month you were born. (Some students may need help with this.)
Write the number of the day you were born.
Write the year you were born.

To make age comparisons, you may need to preteach the comparative form, using only two students.

➤ (to the first student) Say the year you were born.
(to the second student) Say the year you were born.

If you're lucky and they were born in different years, you're set.

➤ (to the two students) Write this sentence on your cards: "(name) is older than (name)."

Now, find two students born in the same year.

➤ (to the first student) Say the year you were born.
(to the second student) Say the year you were born.

You might shrug your shoulders, and say to the class, "Who is older? I don't know."

➤ (to the first student) Say the month you were born.
(to the second student) Say the month you were born.

Write this sentence on your cards: "(name) is older than (name)."

Published by Frank Schaffer Publications. Copyright Protected.   0-7682-3072-1   *Ready, Set, Speak*

If you think that your students will now understand how to determine who is older or younger, make the following a whole-class activity. If your students need further practice, do the activity with four students as a demonstration.

➤ Stand up.
Find a partner.
Stand together. You're a pair.
Look at your partner's card.
Decide who is older.
Write on your card, "(name) is older than (name)."
Now, the two of you find another pair.
All four of you stand together.
Look at everyone's cards.
Write one more sentence on your cards, "(name) and (name) are older than (name) and (name).
Using your sentences, decide who is the oldest, the second oldest, the third oldest, and the youngest.
Make a line.
Put the oldest person on the left.
Put the second oldest person next.
Put the third oldest person next.
Put the youngest person on the right.

After students have had sufficient practice, and assuming that you have some tolerance for chaos, put a sign up on a left-hand wall saying Oldest. Put a similar sign saying Youngest on the right. Stand back, and see if the whole class can arrange themselves from oldest to youngest. Cleverly enough, you have not explicitly taught comparatives (*older*) or superlatives (*the oldest*), but the students have heard the words and understood the relationships. You have taught under the radar, and you can come back to these grammatical structures later.

Once the students have arranged themselves in order, you have identified the fire drill leader, as well as the youngest person, who will have the big responsibility of closing the classroom door. If your school also wants windows closed, perhaps a student in the middle of the line gets that responsibility. Or, if there is more than one window, select a student for each window.

You have established a bank of information that you can use later for direct language instruction. Without paying much attention to it, students have practiced comparatives (*older than*) and superlatives (*the oldest*, the *youngest*).

SCHOOL ORIENTATION

Responding to textbook commands

An enjoyable way to prepare for this lesson is to ask your more advanced students to do some research for a few days. In their other classes, ask them to write down what a teacher says whenever she asks students to refer to a textbook. They'll report back sentences like these:

Open your book.

Open your book to page 97.

Turn to page 97.

Open your book to the third chapter.

Look at the table on page 22.

Look at the next page.

Check the vocabulary list in the back of the book.

Gather a group of such sentences and practice them as commands with your less advanced students.

Learning about the school

Even a small school is a mysterious place for a student new to North American culture. What happens where? Which are the safe places? Are there dangerous places? Learning the functions of various offices as well as the geography of the school is, in microcosm, what students will later encounter in social studies class as they tackle the branches and functions of government, map skills, etc.

Walking around the school is obviously easier with a small group. If you have a large class, enlist the support of parents and/or adults who work in the areas of the school that you plan to visit.

Set the scene. Oh! I see that (Juan) is sick! (You touch his forehead, pulling your hand away to indicate that he is burning up with fever.) We need to take him to the nurse. Gently guiding the "sick" Juan, give the following commands.

> Everyone, quickly stand up.
> Go to the door.
> (to one student) Please open the door.
> (to the rest of the class) Follow me.
> Turn right.
> Walk down the hall.
> Turn right again.
> Go to Room 102.
> Look in the door.
> Alicia, take Juan inside.
> Say, "Juan is sick."

Enlist the nurse's help; the nurse says:

> **Come in, Juan.**
> **Sit here.**
> **Oh, yes, you look sick. (She feels his forehead.)**
> **Go over there and lie down.**

The same drama can be repeated with other students vying to be sick.

On another day, review the commands that tell students how to get to the nurse's office. Now they can draw simple maps indicating their classroom, the halls, and the nurse's office.

Continue posing common student problems: a lost bus pass, disappearing lunch money, arriving late to school, needing permission to leave early, needing to call home. Slowly, over the course of several days, students navigate and renavigate the halls, learning the school through physical movement and formalizing that information on their maps. They have made school a friendlier place and have gained a greater sense of control over their school world.

In addition to creating individual maps, small groups can create a larger map of the school. Letting their fingers do the walking, some students give commands and others "walk" around the school.

1.2 Everyday Routines

Carrying out commands relating to everyday activities can be easy, fun, and often amusing, depending on teachers' and students' creativity.

GETTING READY FOR SCHOOL

Getting up in the morning

Choose a student who is a bit of a ham and tell the class that he's in his bedroom. Put two chairs mostly together to form a bed, and carry on.

> **Lie down on your bed.**
> **Close your eyes. You're asleep.**
> **Ringgggg! The alarm just went off. Open your eyes.**
> **Rub your eyes with your hands.**
> **Shake your head.**
> **Forget it, you're too sleepy. Hit the "snooze" button on your alarm.**
> **Lie down again.**
> **Cover your head with your pillow.**
> **Ringggg! The alarm went off. Open your eyes again.**

Shake your head.
Hit the "snooze" button on your alarm again.
Lie down.
Snore.

This can be repeated as many times as you and the class would like. Then, consider adding a big sister, big brother, or parent who comes in and hauls the reluctant student out of bed.

Getting dressed

This series of commands obviously has to be adapted, depending on age and gender of the students involved, but it might be something like this.

Well! I see you're finally out of bed.
Take off your pajamas. Cold, isn't it?
Put on your underwear.
Put on your socks.
Put on your shirt.
Wait a minute! It's cold today. Take off your shirt.
Put on your sweatshirt.
Put on your jeans.
Put on your sneakers.
Walk to the kitchen.
Fall down. You forgot to tie your sneakers!

If clothing words are new to your students, you could start by dressing a doll.

This first series of commands assumes a fairly normal morning routine. As students begin to respond to the commands more readily, mix them up!

Well, I see you're finally out of bed.
Take off your pajamas.
Walk to the kitchen.
Wait a minute! Please, put some clothes on! Put on your underwear.
Put on your jeans.
Put your sweatshirt over your head.
Put your socks on your feet.
Put your sneakers over your socks.
Good! You're ready for school.

Few students will be able to resist giving outrageous commands to their classmates. I leave this to your imagination, and theirs, and hope that the results are socially acceptable.

FOOD

Both preparing food and eating are activities that can be demonstrated and easily understood. And, of course, they have their own reward if the food is successfully prepared. Two samples appear below. You, your students, and their families can develop similar exercises that bring their own culture into the classroom: eating with chopsticks, eating curries with bread instead of a knife and fork, etc.

Sharing a watermelon

Once, the school's vice principal showed up at a colleague's classroom door with a big watermelon. They invited him in, and he placed the watermelon on a piece of plastic that he had brought. He then took out a long sharp knife—reminding students that, as vice principal, he could bring a knife to school but that they shouldn't. He sliced the watermelon and handed it out, along with napkins, to the surprised and happy students.

The next day, sadly, there was no real watermelon, so the teacher had to pretend.

> **Pick up the watermelon.**
> **Put some plastic under it.**
> **Take out the knife.**
> **Slice a piece of watermelon.**
> **Put it on a napkin.**
> **Give it to (name).**

The commands and responses can be extended to eating the watermelon, spitting out seeds, etc. Very likely, you and the students will extend your imaginary eating to ice cream cones, spaghetti, regional and ethnic delicacies, and to foods specific to holidays. Halloween can provide inspiration as students imagine such goodies as eyeballs, big fat spiders, and more.

Preparing simple foods

Many teachers have designed lessons around actual food preparation. Creating a peanut butter and jelly sandwich is a tried-and-true exercise. Other easy recipes abound in children's cookbooks. As with the watermelon, it is helpful to start with real food. But once the routine is very clear in students' minds (and stomachs), commands carried out without the real thing can be amusing.

➤ Open the bread bag.
Take out two pieces of bread.
Put them on the table.
Open the peanut butter.
Put the knife in the peanut butter.
Put some peanut butter on your nose.
Put some jelly on top of the peanut butter on your nose.
Put one piece of bread on your right ear.
Put one piece of bread on your left ear.
Smile! You're a sandwich!

1.3 A Cat on the Floor

PREPARATION

Create a line drawing of a cat on the floor of the classroom, using whatever drawing material is appropriate. If chalk, pen, or marker is not right for your floor, consider creating the picture with masking tape. Some teachers make semipermanent reusable images out of an old bed sheet or inexpensive shower curtain liner.

    The number of students who can participate at one time depends on the size of your cat and, of course, the size of your students! With a six-foot cat, we might start with three students who respond to the following commands.

➤ Step on its ears.
Step on its tummy/belly/stomach. (You choose which word.)

Step on its nose.
Step on its toes.
Step on its legs.
Step on its eyes.
Step on its mouth.
Step on its tail.
Step on its whiskers.

Save the whiskers command until last, and one of the students may deduce what whiskers are, since all other parts of the cat have already been identified.

Use your preferred way of selecting the next group of students. Practice until every student has had the opportunity to step on the cat's parts or until you think the group's attention is beginning to wander. Though it is desirable for every student to participate, class size may make that impossible. Fortunately, learning also happens through watching and overhearing.

EXPANSIONS AND VARIATIONS

Adding adverbs

It is very likely that some enthusiastic students have stepped on the cat's parts with great enthusiasm. Others may have cringed at the damage done to the poor cat's eyes. Either now or on another day, add two more words.

Step hard on the cat's tail.
Step gently on the cat's eyes.
Etc.

If some students are ready, they can join the teacher in giving commands. As a first step, they may produce only one word, adding either *hard* or *gently* to a command.

Teacher: Step…
Student: …hard…
Teacher: …on the cat's tail.

If you don't have to worry about making too much noise and disturbing other classes, encourage the students to speak the word *hard* quite loudly and *gently* in a soft voice. Coupling action with loudness provides another way for students to learn and remember these two words.

Changing the verb

If you want to encourage your students to be more gentle and peaceful, you could begin with *pat* or *pet* instead of *step on*. Then, of course, the expansion to include *hard* and *gently* is less appropriate.

If you have used *step on* as your introductory command, consider using *pat* or *pet* as a variation, either on the same day or for a later review.

Fortunately for language teachers and learners, body parts sometimes come in pairs. This allows students to become increasingly aware of numbers and singular and plural nouns.

Put one foot on its nose.
Put two feet on its ears.
Etc.

For amusement and a challenge, see how students respond to this command:

Put four feet on its legs.

The clever ones will discover cooperative learning and enlist a classmate to help.

Seatwork

If you haven't yet introduced the word *pat*, now is the time. At their seats, students transfer what they learned from the cat on the floor to human anatomy.

Pat your tummy/belly/stomach.
Pat your ears.
Pat your nose.
Etc.

BEYOND CATS

Some time later, create another animal on the floor. An elephant, for example, invites learning *trunk* and *tusks*. Some students may also be ready to hear that elephants and people have *feet* but cats and dogs have *paws*.

If you and your students enjoy using the floor to walk around and learn things, consider expanding into other subject areas. Build a simple representation of the continents and oceans, traveling quickly from east to west, from north to south.

1.4 Drawing and Building

CREATE WHAT I SAY

Warming up

Start this series of activities by giving the commands with students responding either individually, in pairs, or in small groups. As they are learning the process, "cheating"—looking at what others are doing—is fine.

➤ Take everything off your desk.
  Put one pencil on your desk.
  Put two pieces of paper on your desk.
  One book.
  Take off your right shoe.
  Put it on the desk.
  Now, put your pencil in your shoe.
  Put one piece of paper under your shoe.
  Put the other paper in your book.
  Put your book on your head.

If some students are ready to generate commands, they can work with the same materials in small groups. Groups of three are especially fun. One student gives commands, another follows, and the third watches and giggles over misunderstandings or, more helpfully, assists the student who is following the commands.

Draw a monster

Moving now from actual objects to pencil and paper, give a series of commands that will result in a simple monster. As you give the commands, draw your own picture on an overhead projector, but don't let the students see it yet. At the end of the process, reveal your drawing so that students can check their own.

➤ Let's draw a monster.
  Take out a pen or pencil.
  Take out a piece of paper.
  Draw a circle on your paper for the monster's face.
  The monster has one eye at the top of its face. Draw its eye.
  It has three eyes at the bottom of its face. Draw them.
  It has no nose and no mouth.
  But it has a lot of ears. Draw seven ears on top of its head.
  Draw a long neck.

Draw a circle under its neck for its body.
It has no arms, but it has five legs. Draw the five legs.
It has a foot on one leg, but not on the other four.
Isn't he scary?

Students will eagerly create their own monsters. They can then direct classmates to duplicate their own drawings, working in pairs, triads, or small groups.

Elaborating the process

After the students are very comfortable with this series of commands, add a level of abstraction by using plastic or wooden rods of various colors and lengths. The person who gives commands arranges the rods at the same time that he gives the commands. But his pattern is hidden behind a tall, wide book or a manila folder. Now the process becomes especially enjoyable for the third person—the observer—because he can see each mistake as it is made.

For this sequence, make sure that students know the words *perpendicular* and *parallel* (see the end of this chapter).

Take one orange rod.
Take one pink rod.
Take one blue rod.
Take one brown rod.
(to the observer) Does he have an orange rod, a pink rod, a blue rod, and a brown rod?

If the observer agrees, the sequence continues. If not, they repeat the instructions until it's right.

Put the orange rod perpendicular to the edge of the table nearest you.
(to the observer) Is it right?
Put the blue rod to the left of the orange rod.
Make sure it's parallel to the orange rod.
(to the observer) Are we OK?
Put the brown rod to the right of the orange rod.
Make sure it's perpendicular to the orange rod.
Make sure it touches the bottom of the orange rod.
(to the observer) Are we still OK?
Put the pink rod to the left of the blue rod.
Make sure it's perpendicular to the blue rod.
Make sure it touches the bottom of the blue rod.

At the beginning, it's a good idea to have the student giving commands check periodically with the observer. It can be frustrating to end up with a structure that bears no resemblance whatever to the desired structure. Also, by checking as they progress, the observer can assist the student giving the commands in giving more careful instructions and can assist the builder in understanding those instructions. The observer may not touch the rods, however.

DRAWING GEOMETRY

Demonstrating terms

(Standing up as straight as you can, you say) vertical
(You or a willing student lies down.) horizontal
(Lean as far as you can without falling over.) diagonal

Once the meaning of these three words is clear, students can confirm their understanding and practice the new words by responding to commands individually or as a whole group, and, before long, by giving commands themselves.

From bodies to drawing

Next, extend the practice by drawing lines. Start with simple commands, drawing your own line as you speak. (A word about "cheating": Students are learning, not being tested. If they need to check what a neighbor is doing, let them.)

Draw a horizontal line.

After the students finish, reveal your own line. Continue the same process of command, followed by checking answers, and then the next command.

Draw 3 horizontal lines.
Draw a vertical line.
Draw a diagonal line.
Draw 2 diagonal lines.

With the last command, the responses get interesting, and they set the stage for learning new terms. Perhaps your 2 diagonal lines look like this.

Or perhaps like this.

Or even like this.

See how many ways your students drew their lines and celebrate their diverse answers. If no one has proposed an X, mention it now as another correct answer.

The addition of two words—first *parallel* and later *intersecting*—allows your commands to be more precise. Demonstrate *parallel.* Probably the quickest and easiest way is to draw lines. Then follow with a little practice. You could ask two volunteers to draw each command on the board as you give it. These two student models provide support for students who are unsure, while confident students will tend to ignore the people at the board until they have first drawn their own. The two volunteers can compare and correct their own work as they go, and classmates will no doubt readily point out any errors that they make.

          0-7682-3072-1   *Ready, Set, Speak*

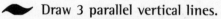 Draw 3 parallel vertical lines.
Draw 4 parallel diagonal lines.
Draw 7 parallel horizontal lines.
Draw 2 horizontal lines and draw 1 vertical line above them.
(Mime "above" if you think it is necessary.)
Draw 1 vertical line and 3 horizontal lines below them. (Again, mime "below" if needed.)

When students have understood and practiced *parallel*, add *intersecting*. Refer to the X that they have already seen, show the point at which they cross, and give them the new word. It's also a good idea at this point to show a number of intersecting lines, because with only the X as an example, students may assume that an intersection happens only at the midpoint of two lines.

It is likely that at this point some students will be eager to give their own commands—if not to the entire class, at least within small groups. Consider using triads instead of pairs, with one student giving the command, a second student responding, and a third person observing and mediating any disputes or asking you for a final ruling. If you want the three students to exchange roles, the observer can also hold a simple egg timer, giving each person three minutes in one role.

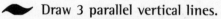 Draw a horizontal line.
Draw a diagonal line intersecting it at any point.
Draw a second horizontal line.
Draw a vertical line intersecting it at any point.
Draw a vertical line.
Draw a horizontal line that intersects it at its midpoint.
Draw a vertical line.
Draw a horizontal line perpendicular to it.

Pay special attention to the last command, because a perpendicular line does not have to fall at the midpoint.

Back to the bodies

Together with the students, create a list of all the terms that students have learned and ask the students to copy them for reference for this next activity. Then, divide the class into small groups. Their challenge, using the bodies of the group members, is to demonstrate each of the terms. More inhibited students can use arms rather than entire bodies. Depending on the age of students, it may be wise to create single-sex groups.

For a concluding performance, each group (or if your class is large, several volunteer groups) presents its terms for the entire class. Each group should display one term, such as *perpendicular*, before proceeding to the next term so that all may appreciate the various ways one term can be represented. If possible, bring a camera because these pictures can become cue cards for further review and expansion. In addition, they make wonderful exhibits for a hall display—with, of course, the actors' permission.

Later on, use a similar process to show angles (*acute, right, obtuse*) and shapes (*rectangles, squares, circles*, various *triangles*).

Language elements

Comparatives (*is older than...*)	1.1
Numbers	
cardinal (*one, two, three...*)	1.3, 1.5
ordinal (*second, third...*)	1.1
Adjectives (colors)	1.5
Dates (January 16, 1995)	1.1
Location and direction (*under, right, parallel, on the left*)	1.4
Singular and plural nouns	
regular (*eye/eyes*)	1.1
irregular (*foot/feet*)	1.1
Vocabulary	
clothing	1.2
foods	1.2
animal and human bodies	1.3

Resources

Asher, James J. *Learning Another Language Through Actions*. Los Gatos
  (CA); Sky Oaks Productions, 2003.
  The classic reference on the theory and practice of Total Physical Response
  (TPR).

Strichez, Gregory. *Before the Bell Rings*. Hayward (CA): Alemany Press,
  1982.
  This is a classic compilation of simple commands to which students
  respond with pencil and paper. The commands include spelling, numbers,
  words, and mathematics practice.

Chapter 2

Visualizing Language

In language, we usually think of words and their parts as the signs that convey sounds and meaning. In teaching language, however, we can create visuals for these signs that are more engaging and memorable for students and that, therefore, facilitate their learning. Such visuals can include gestures, posters, props, color-coded cards, colored pieces of wood, and many other readily available resources. Among the best visuals for teaching and learning, though, are the students' bodies themselves, made to stand for the words, sounds, symbols, punctuation marks, and meanings of language.

Students can use and follow visual signals either at their seats or as they move physically around the room. You and your students have probably already developed a number of visuals that are unique to your class. This chapter will provide many more that you can specifically apply to learning aspects of language.

The activities in this chapter are grouped into broad, though not mutually exclusive, categories. Some may take days to complete and will benefit from review and elaboration. Others may be completed in a matter of moments.

2.1 Sentence Stand-Ins

HUMAN SENTENCES

Students quickly understand and enjoy activities in which one student stands for a word (or a punctuation item). Once they see how moving around illustrates different types of sentences as well as word and spelling changes within sentences, they are eager to create and recreate language with their bodies.

Word order

Many languages place the color word (adjective) after the noun, as in
I want a shirt red.

Before this exercise, prepare six large cards: *I, want, a, shirt, red,* and
a sixth card showing a period. Give the six cards, at random, to six
students.

- If your card says *want*, come to the front of the room.
  Show everyone your card.
  If your card says *shirt*, come to the front of the room.
  Show everyone your card.

Continue this process until everyone except the student with the
red card is in the front of the room.

- (to the assembled five students) Look at everyone's cards.
  Move around until you make a sentence.
  (to the first student) Read your card. (If they are assembled
  correctly, it will be *I.*)

Continue until each student has read his card, and the sentence is
correct. Students are usually quite creative about the sounds they make
to express punctuation.

- Now, hide your cards and read your sentence again.
  Again.
  Faster.

The six students will increase in fluency as they repeat the sentence.
Probably the class will also want to "read" the human sentence. Now,
it's time to add the important word, *red.*

- *Red,* please come to the front.
  Sentence people, decide where red belongs.
  Put red in the right place. (Guide them as needed.)
  Everyone, read your sentence.
  Again.
  Again.
  Faster.

The same process works for the position of other adjectives.

If your students are ready for it, they can also use human sentences to
learn about adverbs, though adverbs are more mobile and therefore

more complicated than adjectives. For example, the adverb *slowly* could go in various places in the sentence *He walks slowly to school: Slowly, he walks to school; He slowly walks to school; He walks slowly to school;* and *He walks to school slowly.*

Using cards with such adverbs as *quickly, happily, sadly, eagerly,* and even *reluctantly,* encourage students to play with human sentences. The movement of an adverb student into and out of the possible slots will help students develop a feel for this mobility.

Making simple negatives

Some sentence types and grammatical structures are more understandable when they are analyzed and manipulated. Students enjoy this activity and find it easy to do, as long as they start with a relatively simple structure.

In this exercise, students continue to form human sentences, using the same process as outlined for creating their first sentence with the color word *red.* This time, prepare seven cards: *she, is, eleven, years, old,* and *n't.* The seventh card has a big dot on it, representing a period.

This time, invite all but the *n't* student to the front of the room and ask them to figure out how to stand in order to make a statement. They should move around, guided by you and the class, until the sentence is correct: *She is eleven years old.* Then bring up the *n't* student and ask the class to point to where she belongs. Once she is in place, the sentence students should read the sentence aloud a few times, followed by the whole class. Often the *is* and *n't* students spontaneously decide to join hands, which makes good sense. If they don't join on their own accord, you can suggest it.

There are a variety of ways to involve the rest of the class. Sometimes the students who formed the original sentence hand their cards to classmates, who then have to reform the sentences at the front of the room. Other times, the original students stay in the front and the rest of the class "reads" them aloud.

On another day, this exercise can be built around some (not all) of

the following grammatically simple variations.
can to *can't*
are to *aren't*
would to *wouldn't*
etc.

A slightly more complex variation involves the shift from *will* to *won't*.

More difficult negatives

On yet another day, you could tackle the third person singular *s* (as in *she likeS*). This s is a continuing challenge for many students. And just when they are starting to remember to use it, it disappears.
He *likes* strawberries.
He *doesn't like* bananas.

To create human sentences for this structure, you will need five cards for the first sentence: *he, like, s, strawberries,* and another period. You will also need two additional cards for the second sentence: *doesn't, bananas.*

As in the previous examples, start with the affirmative structure, making sure that the students you select for *like* and *s* are likely to agree to hold hands.

After the five students can produce the affirmative sentence relatively fluently, continue to use commands to replace the *strawberries* student with the *bananas* student. Bring up the *doesn't* student. Place him properly. Then you have a choice of how to proceed. Your choice depends partly on your assessment of what your students know and how you feel about allowing a "wrong" sentence to stand, at least temporarily.

If you're willing to go with a wrong sentence, you can let the students "read":
He doesn't likes bananas.

You can then wait, seeing if anyone notices a problem. If they don't, of course you do, and with horror you quickly uncouple the *s* student from his partner, *like,* and remove *s* from the line. Students then recite their correct sentence several times.

Or, if you don't want the wrong sentence to be uttered at all, remove the *s* student at the same time that you add the *doesn't* student.

Add some drama. If you have been able to choose your students for their lack of inhibitions, you can now instruct them to read their negative sentence with whatever expressions of abhorrence they can produce. (The more feeling that learners associate with language, the better it is likely to be retained.)

After a few performances of the *doesn't like* form, you quickly instruct the *bananas* and *doesn't* students to leave and the *s* and *strawberries* students to return. Now, of course, the sentence should be read with suitable expressions of pleasure.

Personalize. With the help of students, create a list of fruits and vegetables on the board, with illustrations as needed. Ask students to say which ones they like and which ones they do not like. Note their preferences on the board. If you have a nice poster of fruits and vegetables or if you can create a poster on newsprint that can be used again in the future, consider giving students a set number of sticky notes. Ask them to write their name on each note and then place their name on the appropriate food. If they like the food, the sticky note should also have a smiley face or other such indication. If they don't like it, a frown, perhaps a word like *yuck,* or some other age-appropriate utterance should be used.

Now students can create their own true sentences about their preferences and those of their classmates. If you don't mind competition, put them in small groups, set a time limit, and see who can produce the greatest number of true sentences within a specified time.

Questions

Having formed negatives, your human sentences can go on to form questions. Questions present the same difficulties as negatives so, once again, it makes sense to start with questions that require minimal changes in form, such as:

She can ride a bike.

Can she ride a horse?

On another day, you can remind students of the function of *do* and *does* for negatives, and they'll quickly see what has to happen with questions.

She knows Arabic.

Does she know Spanish?

Published by Frank Schaffer Publications. Copyright Protected.

In these cases, too, students enjoy personalizing the language. With the class, make a list of things that various class members know and can do, making sure that the selected verbs are understood by all.

Tag endings

Human sentences prove their worth when the class is tackling a particularly difficult structure. After they have learned simple question forms, students need to encounter a prevalent but difficult way to make questions—by adding a tag at the end of a sentence.

She is beautiful, isn't she?
You like chocolate cake, don't you?
He can play soccer well, can't he?

Many other languages have "tag endings" to ask questions, but the same phrase is used, regardless of how the sentence begins. For example, Spanish has *verdad*. French has *n'est ce pas*. The closest equivalent English has to a one-size-fits-all tag ending is the colloquial *right*, as in:

You take the bus home from school, right?

English is complicated, because the form of the tag ending depends on the earlier part of the sentence. It can be demystified through the same human sentences process that students have used for easier structures.

Prepare seven cards: she, is, beautiful, n't [.], [,], [?]

Is, please come to the front.
Beautiful, please come to the front.
She, please come to the front.
Pzt (or some other sound representing a period), please come to the front.
Look at each other's cards.
Move around so that you have a sentence.
Hide your cards.
Read your sentence.
Again.
Again.
Faster.

Now, let's make a question. *Question mark*, please come to the front.
Period, please go back to your chair.
OK, group, make yourself into a question.
Hide your cards.
Read your sentence.

Either the *question mark* student or anyone else in the class can propose an appropriate sound to differentiate it from a period.

Now it's time to introduce the tag. Assuming that this is a new concept for the students, you will have to move the actors around a bit at first.

Question mark, please go back to your chair.
Period, please return to the front.
Group, read your sentence. (They read, "She is beautiful[.]")
Comma, come up to the front.
Period, move out of the sentence.
Comma, stand where *period* was.
Is person, stand after *comma*.
N't person, please come to the front.
Is and *n't*, please hold hands
Question mark, come back and stand at the end.
She please move to between *isn't* and *question mark*.
You four, please read your part of the sentence ("[,] isn't she [?]")

The most important thing to understand about tag questions is that certain words appear twice. Students understand this concept as they see their classmates being moved around. Give the following commands and move the students to the appropriate places.

Let's make the whole question. *She*, move back to the beginning.
Is, let go of *n't* and move next to *she*.
Beautiful, you're next to *is*.
Comma, you're next.
Read that part of the sentence only. ("She   is   beautiful   [,]")
Now *is*, move back next to *comma*, and hold *n't's* hand again.
She, run to the place next to *isn't*.
Question mark, you go at the end.
Now read the rest of the sentence ("isn't she [?]")
Are you ready to read the whole sentence? *She* and *is*, run back to your beginning places.
Now read the whole sentence.

She and *is* will quickly discover that halfway through the sentence reading, they must run to their slots toward the end of the sentence. The students will see the pattern—the fact that both *she* and *is* repeat. There is a small refinement of understanding that will be needed if students are then writing these human sentences. *She* is capitalized in the place where it begins a sentence, but not in the second occurrence, where it is part of the tag.

It's just a matter of time before someone produces the inverse:
She isn't beautiful, is she?

RODS INSTEAD OF HUMAN BEINGS

Wooden or plastic modular teaching rods provide more abstract
representations of the same concepts. For follow-up to any of the
human sentence activities, you can distribute a small set of these
colorful blocks to each student or pairs of students. Together with the
students, decide what each rod stands for. Then write the color and
corresponding word or punctuation mark on the board. For example,
the class might decide on these correspondences:
she=dark green
is=red
beautiful=blue
comma=yellow
n't=pink
question mark=brown
period=beige

As you dictate the following, create the sentence yourself. Students
who need help understanding your instructions will, therefore, have
your model to follow.

Pick up the dark green rod. Remember it's *she*.
Put it on your table on your left.
Pick up the red rod. Remember it's *is*.
Put the red rod to the right of the green rod.
Pick up the blue rod. Remember it's *beautiful*.
Put the blue rod to the right of the red rod.
Pick up the beige rod. It's the *period*.
Put it at the end of your sentence.
Now, read your sentence. (Students read, "She is beautiful
period.")
Again.
Again.
Faster.

Now remind students that they have two unused rods, the pink *n't* and

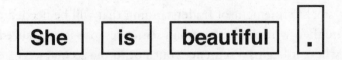

the brown *question mark*. Either individually or in small groups, ask them to create a question that incorporates those additional rods. If they have learned tag endings well during the human sentences exercise, this task should be manageable.

Creating a sentence with a tag ending would look like this.

Notice that the students have placed their punctuation marks vertically to differentiate them from words.

| She | is | beautiful | , | is | n't | she | ? |

From rods to writing

Listening generally comes before speaking—understanding comes before production. In the human sentences activities, students must speak their single words or punctuation marks. After you have done some of the preceding exercises, students will undoubtedly be muttering to themselves as they move rods around. Now is a good time to transform understanding to writing.

Using the rods for an example, recall that you and your students created a key in which words and punctuation marks were represented by colors. It should be easy for students to create a sequence of rods and write the corresponding sentence. The only challenge might be capitalization of the first word of the sentence, though usually just pointing it out is sufficient.

When it is time to write, you might decide to give them two *she* rods and two *is* rods so that the sentences are fully coded without movement. Having nonmoving sentences can be easier for some students at this point.

Personalizing the rods

The blue rod has meant *beautiful* up to now. What other words might students want to describe people? Create a list, using student-volunteered or requested words. Perhaps you will get words like *ugly, lazy, late, tall,* and *handsome.* (After the students have done Cinderella in Chapter 3, they will have an even richer inventory of words.) Now the blue rod can signify a variety of descriptive words.

Having added their own descriptive words, do students want to replace *she* with *he*? The same dark green rod can stand for *he*.

Some students will want to extend their communication further. Both Juan and Lena are tall, so students need *they*. No problem. That dark green rod can be many pronouns. But now, students need *are* to accompany *they*, but they have only *is*. Because the difference between *is* and *are* is a very important one, it's better not to let the red rod do double duty. Select a new color for *are*—perhaps black or orange.

On other days, similar additions can be made for *do, does*, or *did*. It never ends.

2.2 Tune-Up Gestures

GESTURES

Almost without thinking, we use gestures to tell students to speed up, slow down, speak, be quiet, to think more carefully, and much more. Some gestures can be invented for a specific language learning purpose, becoming part of the class culture and providing quick and unobtrusive ways to point out an element of language.

Gestures seem so natural that we tend to think of them as universal. They may not be; a hand gesture that is perfectly acceptable in one culture may have an entirely different (and not necessarily pleasant) meaning in another. So, when you use gestures, be alert for student response. At the same time, it's good for students to understand gestures that are a natural part of your repertoire, even when such gestures may make them feel uncomfortable.

An advantage of gestures is, of course, the fact that they are quick, allowing students and teachers to concentrate on the message and not exclusively on form. And because they are unspoken, they can also be ignored if the student wishes. Often students know best how many elements of language they can attend to at one time.

Grammar and pronunciation gestures

In addition to standard gestures like "thumbs up" and "thumbs down," teachers invent gestures for a specific purpose that may be unique to their class. Many other such gestures are quickly borrowed and spread far and wide. One colleague in Japan uses a series of gestures that point to specific and frequent grammatical misses. He calls these gestures his "friendly non-verbal corrections."

1. Students confuse *he, she* and *him, her*. He places his hand flat out in front of him, and then wiggles it gently back and forth, meaning *that doesn't sound quite right. Try another pronoun.* When they get it right, he gives a "thumbs up."

                    0-7682-3072-1   *Ready, Set, Speak*

2. To indicate that the student needs past, present, or future, he points backward over his shoulder for past, down in front of him in a "now" gesture for present, and slightly forward for future.
3. For the perennial omissions of *s* on the verbs connected with *he, she,* or *it* (the third person singular), he holds up three fingers.

Gestures along with vocal signs can also tune up pronunciation. For students who have trouble with *gr-*, substituting *gl-*, you can make lion or tiger noises—long "grrrrrrr" noises, and make your hand look like a claw. Students will come to associate the *gr-* sound and the clawing gesture with the problem. Eventually, either one will remind them to check their pronunciation.

Finding more gestures

Students are anthropologists all the time though they don't often recognize it. Capitalize on their powers of observation. Start by watching a snippet of a sitcom or other television show with the sound off. Students tell you to stop whenever they see a gesture that they think is worth interpreting. A series of commands initiated by the students might include these:

> **Stop the tape!**
> **Go back.**
> **Play it again.**

The student then repeats the gesture, and the class thinks about what it might mean.

It is only a small step from watching television to observing the real world. Send a few students to the cafeteria to record gestures. If you do not have the courage to assist them in interpreting all of the gestures that they may notice, tell them to ask a good friend.

SILENT TEACHERS

It's time to create a silent teacher when you go home after school, muttering to yourself, "If I've said that once, I've said it a thousand times. I feel like a broken record." The silent teacher is simply a prop or teacher- or student-prepared poster that serves as a quick reminder. You (or vigilant students) can simply point to the silent teacher when needed, rather than stopping to give a spoken reminder. Silent teachers are especially handy when you have laryngitis.

Pronunciation and grammar

The classic silent teacher is a simple teacher- or student-drawn poster of an S, or an S hanging by a string from the ceiling. Teachers or students point to it to remind students of plurals or the third-person singular form (*she writes* rather than *she write*).

Another pronunciation silent teacher might address the pronunciation of past tense verbs with –*ed*. They are all spelled the same, but pronounced differently.

-t   as in *walked, talked*
-ed   as in *repeated, deleted*
-d   as in *cried, lied*

Initially, your silent teacher might appear with examples, and later on it might be more sparse.

-t
-ed
-d

A persistent misuse of a single word can be the occasion for a silent teacher. In one class, students constantly said, "I seen," instead of "I saw." The first silent teacher simply said, "I saw." It was later replaced by a drawing of a saw. (Not coincidentally, students and teacher later adopted a sawing gesture as a reminder.)

Silent teachers don't have to be posters. Again addressing the perennial problem of the missing s, one mischievous colleague keeps a plastic snake handy and waves it at the student who needs a reminder. What does a snake say? Sssssssss, of course.

Subject matter information

For students who have trouble differentiating between city, state, and country, three concentric circles can help. The outside one says *country,* the middle *state,* and the inside one says *city.* Eventually those labels disappear, and the new, refined silent teacher is merely three concentric circles.

Students also enjoy constructing timelines that eventually cover all four walls of the classroom. And as they begin to see the usefulness of silent teachers, students themselves may suggest other topics.

Classroom behavior

A colleague once admitted that she had used silent teachers for other less lofty purposes as well. One day, noting her exasperation with one particularly chatty classmate, her students suggested that she create a silent teacher that read, "Edwin, please stop talking." She did, and the poster was successful in a number of ways: It saved her voice, affirmed that everyone in the class understood the problem that Edwin was creating, and, because it was done with gentle humor, Edwin understood and tried to moderate his side commentary.

Instead of a sign, the silent teacher could have been a simple smiley face with a zipper in place of a mouth. As such, it would support teaching the expression "zip it up" as well as being applicable to all the noisy little Edwins in the class.

2.3 Coded Cards

QUICK ASSESSMENT AND FEEDBACK

Whenever possible, give students the opportunity to think about how well they are doing, how much they are understanding. As they develop the ability to judge themselves, the teacher no longer performs that role exclusively, and students move closer to becoming fully responsible learners. If they have not fully grasped a concept, it's better to know it at the time, and to give them the power to say, "Hey, wait a minute!"

Color-coded cards offer you the opportunity to see how your students are assessing their own understanding. Students prepare their own cards, small enough to store easily but large enough to be seen. They use the three standard traffic colors: red, yellow, and green (an opportunity to teach stop, caution, and go if the students have not yet learned these color codes). At the end of a lesson or at any point along the way, you can use these cards to check understanding. With students' eyes closed and the three colors nearby, you say:

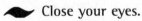 **Close your eyes.**
   Raise the green card if you understand (concept) very well.
   Raise the yellow card if you are pretty sure that you understand it.
   Raise the red card if you're lost!
   Put down your cards.
   Open your eyes.

If "lost" is too idiomatic to be understood, you can always say, "if you don't understand."

As well as identifying students who do not understand, this process also allows you to see how many green cards are showing. Often, behavior problems come from students who are not challenged. Give them a yellow or red partner and watch them shine.

 Close your eyes.
Raise the green card if you understand this so well that you could teach it to someone else.
Raise the yellow card if you are pretty sure that you understand it, but you don't think you could exactly explain it.
Raise the red card if you're lost!
Put down your cards.
Open your eyes.

Now, the green card people have to show that they truly do understand by working as peer teachers in small groups with their yellow and red classmates. Assign each green teacher (or pairs or small groups of green teachers) an area of the class, and invite the rest of the students to go to any green teacher's area. Students who are still learning have saved some pride because they have not publicly identified themselves as red or as yellow—just as not green.

Sorting for learning

Students can use the same three traffic light colors to practice vocabulary or spelling. Having already created small cards with the words they're learning, they sort them into piles next to the appropriate color. Then they clip or rubber-band each package. At the right time, they bring out their red or yellow cards, review them, and see if any can move to the green package.

It's probably impossible to overemphasize the importance of creating and recreating categories as part of learning. If, for example, students are learning the names of living things, they could have a green card for plants, a blue card for insects, a brown card for reptiles, and then sort the animals that they know. Or they could sort with one color for skin, another for fur, another for feathers. The more different categories you and your students can invent, the more deeply they will understand new words, and the more nimble their minds are likely to become.

SAME OR DIFFERENT?

To check perceptions, make sure the students understand the concept of "same" and "different." For example, hold up two identical books and ask:

➤ **Are these the same or different? Raise your right hand if they're the same.**
Raise your left foot if they're different.

Add a few more examples until you're sure that students understand the meaning of "same" and "different."

After you are sure that students understand these two key words, decide as a group what color will represent "same" and what color will represent "different" (preferably not red, yellow, or green). The students cut or tear their two color-coded cards into whatever shapes they want, and then write "same" or "different" on the appropriate card.

Pronunciation

The uses for these two cards never end. As we look to refine students' pronunciation, an often-overlooked fact is that students will not pronounce a word accurately unless they can first hear it accurately. Hold up pictures, toys, or actual objects to represent *ship* and *chip*. Pronounce each word as you hold up the appropriate object.

➤ **Ship. Chip. Are these two words pronounced the same or differently?**
Hold up the (color) card if they're the same.
Hold up the (color) card if they're different.

You can continue with other *sh- ch-* pairs, such as *share* (pantomiming the concept of share) /*chair, sheet/cheat* (*Cheat* is a word students tend to learn early.), etc. You will discover your students' pronunciation problem best by listening and using the examples that you hear from them.

If you want students to move around more, try something like this:

➤ **itch, each**
If they sound the same, put the (color) card in your right hand and run to the right side of the room.
If they sound different, put the (color) card in your left hand and run to the left side of the room.
If you're not sure, stand up, hold both colors, and turn around and around.

0-7682-3072-1   *Ready, Set, Speak*

By these simple actions, if the students are able to be honest about how they hear the words, you have created a group of students who hear the difference and two other groups who do not. You have created a nice setup for more peer teaching and practice.

Vocabulary

Same/different cards can serve many other purposes besides pronunciation. For example, if you are preparing students for a Bingo game that shows fruits and vegetables and you want to practice the words, you could hold up a fruit and a vegetable, asking if they are from the same category or from different categories. Working on science vocabulary, differentiate between mammals and fish, insects and birds, etc. A perennial problem for many students is the difference between city, state, and country. In this case, Paris and Miami would be the same, but France and California would not.

Polite and rude cards

One of the most sophisticated concepts that students need to grasp is that of appropriate language. A good command to start with is one that students have probably already heard in various forms: *Shhhh, Be quiet! Shut up!, Would you mind being quiet?*, or the more indirect *I can't hear!*

Students create the color-coded cards for *polite* and *rude*. There are a number of enjoyable ways to set the scene. If your principal and another colleague are available, invite them into the classroom for a small drama.

➤ (to the principal) Talk loudly to the teacher. (She does.)
(to the teacher) Talk loudly to the principal. (She does.)
(to them both) Keep on talking. (They do.)

Then you stand nearby and start trying to say something to the class. It will quickly become clear that the principal-teacher conversation is annoying you. Look very annoyed. Sigh a lot. Finally say:

➤ Could you please talk more quietly?
(to the principal) Say, "Oh, sure." (She does.)
(to the teacher) Say, "Oh, I'm sorry." (She does.)

Debrief a little, and identify the previous conversation as polite or respectful. Repeat the little drama. If the class has decided that blue equals *polite*, tell them to hold up their blue cards when you speak.

Next, go for contrast. Repeat the same drama, but this time, you say:

 Shut up!
(to the principal) Look surprised and shocked. (She does.)
(to the teacher) Say, "How rude!" (She does.)

Encourage students to hold up the colored card for *rude*—maybe pink.

If the principal and teacher are willing to continue playing, let students hold up cards to cue you and your two other actors to what kind of comment to make. After the students have exhausted the fun of giving orders to three adults, it's likely that many students will be ready to take the places of the three actors.

Formal, informal, and slang

Advanced students who are ready to learn about register and levels of language could use color-coded cards to distinguish among *formal*, *informal*, and *slang* speech. For example:
They were interrogated by the authorities.
The police asked them many questions.
The cops grilled them.

If you use this example, you'll need to explain some of the words. What other examples can you devise? If your students are ready to think about this issue, you can also discuss how the different levels are either appropriate or inappropriate depending on context, audience, and situation. At a football game, for example, they would say, *Rip 'em up, tear 'em up*, rather than *Repel them! Annihilate them!*

As the variations continue, you may create additional scenarios to demonstrate that it can be just as wrong to be too formal as it is to be too informal.

Another useful set of commands for students to understand and use are the "Gimmes": *May I please have..., Could you give me...,* etc. As you listen to your students, you will discover other words and phrases that need to be adjusted, depending on whom the students are talking to and what the current young people's language includes. Recently, *whatever* has been a word that needed explicit attention because students heard it constantly and didn't realize that many adults would consider it rude.

2.4 Visualizing Academic Knowledge

THE HUMAN BAR GRAPH

In social studies classes, students need to interpret information presented in tables and graphs. In mathematics, they have to create graphs. The human bar graph activity presented in this chapter kills three birds with one stone—develops mathematics knowledge, social studies knowledge, and English language.

A natural way to use the information presented in a bar graph is to make comparisons. An easy human attribute to compare is height. The following exercise makes the abstract nature of a bar graph immediately concrete.

Gathering information

➤ Everyone, stand up.
The tallest person, please stand on the left.
The shortest person, please stand on the right.
Everyone else put yourself in the line.

You may need to move a few students around until they get the idea. Once the line is established, pick five students—the shortest, the tallest, and three others in between.

Presenting information

Place five sturdy chairs (all the same size) against a wall, a section of which you have previously covered with newsprint. Invite your five selected students to stand on the chairs and ask other students to mark the top of their heads and the bottom of their feet on the newsprint as follows.

➤ (to the first student) Stand here, on this chair.
(to a classmate who is not one of the five) Take this marker.
Make a horizontal line near the top of [name's] head.
Make another horizontal line near the bottom of [name's] shoes.
Give the marker to another student.

Bring up the remaining four students in any order, and the process continues until all five students' heights are represented.

Now, ask the students who have been measured to step away and represent their height as vertical bars. Say to the five students:

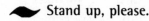 Step away from the wall (gesturing to make your meaning clear, if necessary)
Take a marker.
Draw two parallel vertical lines from the top of your head to the bottom of your shoes.
Under your shoe line, write your name.
Put away the markers.
Put the chairs back.
Thank you. Please sit down.

Next, it's time to take a break and talk about the information that your students' drawing conveys, practicing some useful language at the same time. Gesturing to make your meaning clear, you compare two students, using the bar graph.
Alicia is taller than Tony.
Carlos is taller than Alicia.
Betty?
Tony?
And then they are left with Yasmin. Maybe someone will be able to say, Yasmin is taller than nobody.

Yasmin, the shortest student, provides your opportunity to turn the structure around.
Yasmin is shorter than ....
Alicia is shorter than...

In small groups, students can prepare their own true sentences about as many people in the class as time allows. Looking around the room, they will of course discover that most of their classmates are seated. At any point, a member of the small group can gather data by going over to two classmates, asking them to stand up, and checking their relative heights.

Stand up, please.
Thank you. You can sit down now.

As a final touch on the newsprint, take the marker and draw a horizontal line along the bottom of the bar graph through the horizontal shoe lines. Tell students this is the *x*-axis and it represents people. Then draw a vertical line up the left side of the graph. Tell students that it is the *y*-axis and represents height. Ask them if they have seen graphs giving other information in other classes and encourage them to share. If they have not seen such graphs (or don't remember), tell them to watch for them and to report to the class when they do find them.

Your bar graph should now look like this.

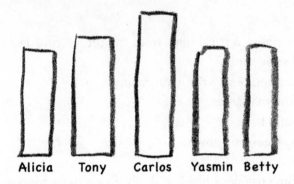

Alicia   Tony   Carlos   Yasmin   Betty

SIGNS FOR MATHEMATICAL OPERATIONS

While they are still learning English, students need to survive in other classes as well. In math class, for example, the student who has painstakingly learned that *2 and 2* are 4, may get completely flustered when the teacher asks him how much 2 *plus* 2 are. Or worse, what 2 *plus 2 equals*. What means *plus*? What means *equal*? I wanna go home!

The same problem can arise when a teacher uses *minus* and *take away* interchangeably or *times* and *multiplied by*. There aren't too many different ways to say *divided by*, and teachers who use such terms as *divisor* and *dividend* probably also say things like *multiplicative property* and can't communicate even with native speakers of English.

The following activity is designed to give students a little more security amid some of the basic language they will encounter in math class. Who knows? Maybe they'll learn a little math. And maybe—just maybe—they'll learn a little algebra.

The equations for this activity are given in order of the categories—addition, subtraction, multiplication, and division—but you can follow a more random order if you choose. It may be wise to do a couple from each category first to allow all students to catch on, then start mixing them up. (Of course, don't tell them the categories until they've come up with the answer.)

Addition	Multiplication
3 ? 6 = 9	3 ? 2 = 6
2 ? 3 = 5	4 ? 2 = 8
1 ? 7 = 8	3 ? 3 = 9

Subtraction	Division
4 ? 3 = 1	8 ? 4 = 2
6 ? 2 = 4	8 ? 2 = 4
9 ? 4 = 5	9 ? 3 = 3

For this activity, you will need cards that students can hold in their hands and that are big enough so that everyone in the class can see what's written on them. They should include the following:
1 card for

each of the numerals 0 through 9

the + symbol and the words *and* and *plus*

the – symbol and the words *minus* and *take away*

the x symbol and the words *times* and *multiplied by*

the ÷ symbol and the words *divided by*

the = symbol and the words *is, are, equal,* and *equals*

2 cards, each for the question mark (?).

You should also write the operations symbols on the chalkboard, along with the corresponding words.

Single-answer operations (a ? b = c)

You will need ten students to hold the cards. Three students will share responsibility for holding the numeral cards. Distribute each of the other cards to one student. Bring all the students to the front of the room.

After the *numeral* students have picked up their numerals, ask them to stand slightly apart so that there is room for other students. Have the five operations students and the two *question-mark* students stand to the side, holding their cards so that everyone can see them.

The procedure for the first addition equation is as follows.

Numeral people, pick up 3, 6, and 9.
Face the class.
3, stand on the class's left.
6, stand to the right of 3.
9, stand to the right of 6.

Now, we need some mathematical signs.
Equals, stand between 6 and 9.
Question mark, stand between 3 and 6.

Ask the students still in their seats to raise their hands when they know which student (from the +, –, x, and ÷ students standing by the wall) should replace the student holding the question mark in the line. (You could also call it the problem, and eventually, the equation. But don't rush it.) Insist that your students not shout or say the answer. Instead, choose one student whose hand is up.

🌿 (to the student who raises her hand) Walk to the front of the
room.
Take the question mark student away.
Choose the plus student and lead him into the empty space.

She could lead the students by the hand, as long as your class is not
at the wrong stage of pre-adolescence. In this case, the student holding
the + symbol card would be the correct response.

Once the correct operations student is in place, have one student or
all the students read the equation aloud. They can try out the different
ways of saying it: "Three and six are nine," "Three plus six equals
nine," etc. You should encourage students to read the variations aloud
so that they settle into the students' ears and vocal cords.

Continue the activity with the other equations. You can also create
and add your own equations to the list, but be careful! As you will see
from the variations of this exercise that follow, some equations may
contain booby traps that you should know about before stepping on
them.

Once your students get the idea and pattern of the exercise, you
can toss them a couple of curve balls and see what happens.

$2 ? 2 = 4$
$5 ? 0 = 5$

You figured it out, didn't you? And it makes you feel kind of proud.
There are two possible answers for each of these.

$2 + 2 = 4$ and $2 \times 2 = 4$
$5 + 0 = 5$ and $5 - 0 = 5$

See if you can coax this revelation from some of your students.
They'll be just as proud as you were. Interestingly, except for any
number multiplied by zero, 2 is apparently the only number in this
whole universe which comes out the same when added to or multiplied
by itself.

Moving the equal sign

The next set of exercises works the same way as the preceding one. The
only difference is that the equal sign student stands between the first
and second number students rather than between the second and third.

In addition to having the students continue to practice speaking
out the equations in their various ways, this exercise will instill in them

the understanding that the equal sign can be in either position, as long as the expressions on either side of it represent the same value.

In addition, this activity will prepare students for the next activity, where things get more complicated.

You should assign different students to the various number and operations card-holding roles so that they can get out of their seats and so that the others can now offer the solutions.

Here is a set of equations you can use for this activity. By now you should be mixing the four operations up rather than doing all addition first, then subtraction, etc.

Addition	Multiplication
7 = 3 ? 4	8 = 2 ? 4
9 = 3 ? 6	9 = 3 ? 3
5 = 2 ? 3	7 = 7 ? 1

Subtraction	Division
7 = 9 ? 2	4 = 8 ? 2
3 = 9 ? 6	2 = 6 ? 3
4 = 5 ? 1	3 = 6 ? 2

By this point in the activity, a couple of things should be happening. First, your students should be growing more and more comfortable with the different ways of expressing addition, subtraction, etc. The repeated practice of reading each solved problem aloud in the various ways it can be read will internalize those variations for your students and make confusion in math class less likely.

Second, your students should begin to be intrigued by some of the things that happen in math, and they should feel some satisfying power in their growing ability to manipulate it to make sense. Involving their bodies in the learning process rather than limiting it to pencil and paper abstractions or vocabulary drills makes the learning process itself more concrete and the outcomes more attainable.

Two-answer operations (a ? b ? c)

This variation follows the same procedure as the previous ones, except that now students will have to place both the operation sign and the equal sign in slots to come up with a correct equation. In this exercise, you will place a *question mark* student between each of the *numeral* students, and the student who raises his or her hand to offer an answer must lead both *question mark* students away, replacing them with an operation student and a = student.

The equations provided for this variation are all the ones provided for the two previous activities.

Because of what they saw in the previous variations of the activity, students should now realize two things.

1. that the equal sign can go in either slot (though not always, as they will see)
2. that there may be more than one correct way to set up the equation.

Here are the equations again, with possible answers printed next to them. Some observations will follow.

Addition	Answers		
3 ? 6 ? 9	3 + 6 = 9		
2 ? 3 ? 5	2 + 3 = 5		
1 ? 7 ? 8	1 + 7 = 8		
7 ? 3 ? 4	7 = 3 + 4	or	7 − 3 = 4
9 ? 3 ? 6	9 = 3 + 6	or	9 − 3 = 6
5 ? 2 ? 3	5 = 2 + 3	or	5 − 2 = 3

Subtraction			
4 ? 3 ? 1	4 − 3 = 1	or	4 = 3 + 1
6 ? 2 ? 4	6 − 2 = 4	or	6 = 2 + 4
9 ? 4 ? 5	9 − 4 = 5	or	9 = 4 + 5
7 ? 9 ? 2	7 = 9 − 2		
3 ? 9 ? 6	3 = 9 − 6		
4 ? 5 ? 1	4 = 5 − 1		

Multiplication

3 ? 2 ? 6	$3 \times 2 = 6$		
4 ? 2 ? 8	$4 \times 2 = 8$		
3 ? 3 ? 9	$3 \times 3 = 9$		
1 ? 5 ? 5	$1 \times 5 = 5$	or	$1 = 5 \div 5$
8 ? 2 ? 4	$8 = 2 \times 4$	or	$8 \div 2 = 4$
9 ? 3 ? 3	$9 = 3 \times 3$	or	$9 \div 3 = 3$
7 ? 7 ? 1	$7 = 7 \times 1$	or	$7 \div 7 = 1$

Division

8 ? 4 ? 2	$8 \div 4 = 2$	or	$8 = 4 \times 2$
8 ? 2 ? 4	$8 \div 2 = 4$	or	$8 = 4 \times 2$
9 ? 3 ? 3	$9 \div 3 = 3$	or	$9 = 3 \times 3$
4 ? 8 ? 2	$4 = 8 \div 2$		
2 ? 6 ? 3	$2 = 6 \div 3$		
3 ? 6 ? 2	$3 = 6 \div 2$		

Why are there two correct answers for some equations and only one for others? The answer appears to be related to syntax. In addition and multiplication, you can read an expression in either direction (left to right or right to left) and it will still be true $(2 + 3 = 3 + 2; 2 \times 3 = 3 \times 2)$. In subtraction and division, however, you cannot do that $(6 - 3 \neq 3 - 6; 6 \div 3 \neq 3 \div 6)$, unless of course the two numbers are the same $(2 - 2 = 2 - 2)$.

This phenomenon may not be relevant to these activities or to your class (unless you choose to bring it up and make something of it). However, it may be helpful for you to be aware that it could be a source of either confusion or insight for a student.

Teachers have often observed that the best, most natural, and least painful way to learn a language is as a by-product of doing something else. In these activities, the students are learning English as a by-product of doing math. Perhaps they are also learning math as a by-product of doing English. It's a win-win situation.

Language elements

Negatives	
simple negatives of verbs *(is, isn't; can, can't)*	2.1
irregular negatives of verbs *(won't)*	2.1
negatives formed by adding *(do, does, did)*	2.1
Questions	
simple questions	2.1
tag questions	2.1

Comparatives	2.4
Register: formality, informality, etc.	2.2
Position of adjectives and adverbs	2.1
Pronunciation	
ship/chip; itch/each	2.3
gr	2.2
third person singular *s*	2.2
simple past tenses	2.2
Pronouns *(he, she/ him, her)*	2.2
Verbs (using present, past, future)	2.2

Resources

Chamot, Anna Uhl and J. Michael O'Malley. *The CALLA Handbook: Implementing the Cognitive Academic Language Learning Approach.* Reading (MA): Addison-Wesley, 1994.
The CALLA Handbook offers even more examples of mathematical language challenges and provides a similar analysis of the challenges that English language learners face in social studies, science, and literature and composition.

Educational Solutions
99 University Place, 2nd Floor
New York, New York 10003-4555
http://members.aol.com/edusol99/index.htm
Educational Solutions is one source of modular teaching rods. They are also available in teacher supply stores or are sometimes packaged as manipulatives with your school's mathematics program.

Acting in the Arena: The Imaginary Real World

You don't have the time or money to take your students out of the classroom and into the real world every day, so you bring the real world into your classroom and set it up in the Arena.

The Arena is the center of your room—all the space that you can create by pushing students' desks against the walls, leaving only as much room for entry and exit as their age and dignity require. The Arena will need to hold anywhere from one to all of your students at a time (if it can), and they'll often be moving about, so make it as big as possible. Students should be able to climb in and out of their seats without stepping on each other too much.

As you progress through the activities of this chapter, the Arena will be transformed from an empty space into a living room, a department store, a television screen, and other such places. It will be full of furniture, fixtures, and equipment—all imaginary, but all very real to you and your students. Once you establish various scenes by going though activities, you will always be able to switch back and forth among them instantly—no heavy lifting, no cumbersome sets, no storage problems for bulky scenery.

The scenarios will develop as you give directions by means of gestures and modeling and as the students respond by carrying out those directions. All (or nearly all) will involve physical activity on the part of the students. You tell four students to lift the couch, and the four of them lift the couch. You tell them to carry it through the door, and they carry it through the door. You show them how to make it seem heavy, and they groan and stagger under its weight.

Before any activity begins, duplicate the reproducible page containing labeled pictures of much of the activity's key components, and give all students a copy for their notebooks. You will also post large labeled pictures of the same components on the walls so you can point to them and students can see them from anywhere in the room. If your principal doesn't greet you at the door each day with fistfuls of money saying, "buy expensive visual materials for the children," have the students themselves draw and label the pictures on newsprint. Do that anyway—better learning experience.

Each activity in the chapter gets you started with the scene and the situation, and it provides a detailed scripting of stage directions (for you), commands or directions (for you to give the students), and student actions. As the activity develops, the scripting becomes less detailed because by then you'll have the idea, and it's likely you and your class will have carried the scenario in your own directions anyway. You could probably carry any of these scenarios on forever, but you should quit and go on to something else when it's no longer productive or no longer fun.

As with most of the activities in this book, do not push your students to speak until they are ready. Let them absorb the language around them through their eyes, their ears, their skin, their bones, and the motion of their bodies for as long as they need. You'll know when they're ready to speak or write; when you see evidence that they're ready, invite it, welcome it, encourage it, and celebrate it. Let the students give commands instead of you. Let them transform the whole scenario if they want. If they're using the language and the activity moves ahead even though you recede, fade away!

Most scenes could appear in more than one activity. The chapter provides suggestions for such activities, but space prohibits spelling them out with detailed scripts. Once you have established locations for the imaginary components of a scene, you'll find that the students can point to those components in the empty Arena weeks or even months later. "There's the sofa, and there's home plate!" "Oh, yeah! I remember!" Once created, the imaginary reality of the Arena will always be there for you and your students.

Stage directions for you are given in parentheses, both before and after the commands. The stage directions indicate whom you are addressing. Continue addressing subsequent commands to that person until another stage direction has you address another person. Some stage directions, along with tips for teaching, are interjected without parentheses.

3.1 The Living Room

PREPARATION

Set up the Arena. Student chairs and desks are pushed back in a horseshoe shape, leaving as much open space in the center of the classroom as possible.

Give students a copy of the living room reproducible page for their notebooks, and ask them to draw larger versions of the labeled pictures for posting so that, ideally, everyone can see them from anywhere in the room. The pictures will contain many of the objects and much of the vocabulary associated with the scenario. The posted pictures will provide visual cues for the student as the scenario goes along.

SITUATION

The class has decided to take a Saturday morning to help a new classmate move into his/her house and set up the living room. Pick one of the students to be the new arrival. To begin, the living room (the Arena) is empty, and the furniture (all imaginary) is on a truck (also imaginary) outside the classroom door (the real door).

Before you begin, review the posted pictures and labels, pointing to them, saying the words, and asking the students to repeat them.

The scenario may be followed as written or varied almost infinitely. Give one command at a time, and wait for it to be followed before giving the next command. Students do not need to say anything. But they are welcome to offer their own suggestions and commands when and if they are ready and want to.

ACTION

Begin by selecting one student to be the door holder, and four others (strapping, strong ones) to be the heavy lifters.

> (to the one) Open the door and hold it open.
> (to the four) Go out to the truck. (They leave the room.)
> (through the door to the four) Lift the sofa. (They do, as you watch through the door. The rest of the class can't see them.)
> Carry it off the truck. (They do.)

~ Bring it into the room. (They enter, carrying the sofa. Coach them to act as if the sofa is heavy.)
(to the class, as the four stand there struggling with the heavy, imaginary sofa) Where should we put it?

Use gestures to convey the question to whatever extent students don't comprehend the words. Students can respond by pointing.

~ (to the four) Put the sofa down over there, next to the window. (Indicate the location of the imaginary window.)
(to the class) Does that look OK? (Some will say no. If not, you say no, and make the four lift it and set it down in two or three more places.)
(to everyone) There! Now it's perfect! (Convey with gestures as needed.)

Send the five students back to their seats. Then say:

~ (to everyone) Uh-oh! We forgot the carpet! (Point to carpet picture.) The carpet goes under the sofa! (Convey by gestures.)
(to the door holder) Come back again and hold the door.
(to the four movers) Lift the sofa again.
Take it out the door and set it down.
Come back in.

Send the five students back to their seats again. Then bring five new students up into the Arena.

~ (to one of them) Hold the door.
(to the other four) Go out to the truck.
Lift the carpet onto your shoulders. (Show them how to hold it on their shoulders.)
Bring the carpet into the living room. (Convey by gestures as necessary.)
Set the carpet down on the floor.
Roll it out. (Congratulate them: "Good job!" or "Very well done!")

Send this group of five back to their seats, and bring the first group of five back into the Arena. Using the original commands, direct the door holder to hold the door again, and the other four to go back out by the truck, pick up the sofa, carry it back in, and put it in place again.

By now, you've got the idea. Once the sofa is placed, choose other students and direct them to bring in and place the other items of furniture: chair, tables, lamps, television, etc. You should be able to get all students involved in sharing this labor of friendship. Your commands will include positional prepositions where they make sense. For example:

> Put the coffee table in front of the sofa on the carpet.
> Put the end table beside the sofa.
> Put the table lamp on the end table.
> Put the floor lamp near the chair.
> Put the television across from the sofa.
> Put the plant under the window.
> Etc.

When the furniture is all in place in the room, have students return to their seats. Then bring eight students up to the Arena.

> (to three of them) Sit on the sofa. (They'll have to squat or sit on the floor.)
> (to a fourth) Sit in the chair.
> (to a fifth and sixth) Stand near the window.
> (to the seventh and eighth) Sit on the carpet in front of the coffee table.

A teachable moment

Because you have teaching embedded in your soul, you can't resist taking advantage of a teachable moment. So with the eight students in the living room and with the rest at their desks, give them all a big smile and announce that this is a wonderful opportunity to learn more English.

If students are able to produce some of the words, point to each separate (imaginary) item of furniture, and the students say its name. If students are not ready to produce, you say each name, and the students point to the correct location. Use the labeled pictures on your walls to help when you need to make clear what an item of furniture is.

Thank-you party

With the eight students still sitting and standing in the living room, bring the new classmate (the one who lives in the house) into the Arena.

> Come into your living room.

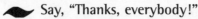 Say, "Thanks, everybody!"
Go to the kitchen. (She goes to the kitchen. It can be through the classroom door, even though that door also leads outside to the truck.)
Pick up the tray with lemonade on it.
Bring the tray back here, into the living room.
Pour a glass of lemonade for each of your helpers.
Say, "Thank you very much for helping me move into my new house!"

FOLLOW–UP

Rearranging small furniture

Arrange the students in groups of two or four around a desk, table, or other shared surface (a miniature Arena/living room), and give each group another copy of the reproducible living room page for this activity. Students cut out the separate pieces of furniture. One student gives commands (as you did), and the other(s) place the furniture as directed in the miniature living room.

Expansion

With students working in pairs, one student describes his living room layout, and the other draws and labels the layout on paper. The partner who described his living room then evaluates the drawing his partner made. Thus they can determine where the communication worked and where it broke down. Then they switch roles and do the same thing.

Prepositions of location

Hold an eraser in one hand and ask students to tell you where it is as you move it to various positions.

On top of your head
Beside your hip
Under your other hand
In front of your nose
Next to your ear
Behind your knee
Etc.

Make your own living room

Students draw and label the furniture layout in their own living rooms and keep the drawing in their notebooks.

Other living room scenarios

You and your students could invent more scenarios to take place in the living room, especially now that it's so nicely furnished. See if the students have ideas.

One possibility is to hold a birthday party for a member of the class. The scenario could include guests arriving, knocking on the door, being let in, opening presents, blowing out candles, eating cake and so on. They could also learn and sing "Happy Birthday."

Before they have a party, however, they should really clean the place, so there's another scenario. Bring in a bunch of students and have them dust, vacuum, sweep cobwebs, wash windows, polish glasses, bake a cake (out in the kitchen), change light bulbs, and so on.

3.2 The Department Store

PREPARATION

For this activity, the Arena will be the clothing section of a department store. Students will be employees (stock and sales) and customers.

Before you begin the activity, give students a copy of the department store reproducible page for their notebooks, and ask them to draw larger versions of the labeled pictures for posting so that everyone can see them from anywhere in the room. The pictures will contain many of the objects and much of the vocabulary associated with the scenario. The posted pictures will provide visual cues for the student as the scenario goes along.

In addition to the labeled pictures you have posted, have on hand a stack of 4 x 6 cards in each of the following colors: blue, red, yellow, and green. (You will need at least 18 cards of each color, for a total of 72 cards.) On each card, have students print the name of the color of the card in big letters. Then, have students write S (for small), M (for medium), or L (for large) on the cards. You should end up with one card for each color and each size for each item of clothing. This chart shows the distribution of colors and sizes.

	Blue	Red	Yellow	Green
S	boys' shirts	boys' shirts	boys' shirts	boys' shirts
M	boys' shirts	boys' shirts	boys' shirts	boys' shirts
L	boys' shirts	boys' shirts	boys' shirts	boys' shirts
S	boys' jeans	boys' jeans	boys' jeans	boys' jeans

M	boys' jeans	boys' jeans	boys' jeans	boys' jeans
L	boys' jeans	boys' jeans	boys' jeans	boys' jeans
S	baseball hats	baseball hats	baseball hats	baseball hats
M	baseball hats	baseball hats	baseball hats	baseball hats
L	baseball hats	baseball hats	baseball hats	baseball hats
S	blouses	blouses	blouses	blouses
M	blouses	blouses	blouses	blouses
L	blouses	blouses	blouses	blouses
S	skirts	skirts	skirts	skirts
M	skirts	skirts	skirts	skirts
L	skirts	skirts	skirts	skirts
S	girls' jeans	girls' jeans	girls' jeans	girls' jeans
M	girls' jeans	girls' jeans	girls' jeans	girls' jeans
L	girls' jeans	girls' jeans	girls' jeans	girls' jeans

Tape your labeled pictures of the six items of clothing in a nice row across the chalkboard. (The other labeled pictures can go anywhere.) In the chalk tray below each clothing picture, place a stack of cards containing one card for each color and size. You are now ready to roll.

ACTION

Bring two or three students up to the front of the room. Pin a name tag on their clothing to communicate that they are employees of the store.

❧ Go into the back room. (Gesture them out through the classroom door and into the hall.)
Roll in the rack of boys' jeans. (Gesture them back in, rolling the imaginary rack.)
Place it here. (Have them line it up perpendicular to the chalkboard and in front of the Boys' Jeans sign.)
Well done!

Send this group back to their chairs, bring up two or three more, and direct them similarly.

❧ Go into the back room. (They do.)
Roll in the table of boys' shirts. (They do.)
Place it here. (in front of the Boys' Shirts sign)

Continue the process with different students until racks of all six items of clothing are in place under their respective labels on the chalkboard.

Say to the students, "Now we need to clean the store."

Bring seven new students into the Arena.

> (to two of them) Take these brooms. (Give them the imaginary brooms.)
Sweep the floor. (Demonstrate *sweep* if you need to. They begin sweeping.)

While the two are sweeping, assign another to dust the changing room. The changing room can be just outside the classroom door (like the back room) or in a corner of the Arena itself.

> (to a third, the duster) Here, take this dust rag. (Give him the rag.)
Dust the changing room. (Model the activity through gestures.)
(to a fourth) Take this bottle of window cleaner and this rag. (Give him the items.)
Clean the mirror. (Show him how to do it.)
(to the fifth) Take this rag and dust the sales counter.
(to the sixth and seventh) Straighten up the clothing on the racks. (Show them how.)
Straighten up the clothing on the tables.

When they are finished, feel free to repeat, end, or expand the activity. You may decide that the cleaners did not do a good enough job, so a different group of students may have to come up and repeat it (hearing all the commands and connecting them with the actions once again).

Students do not really need to speak at all for this activity to work. But any time they show they are ready or eager, encourage them by having them give some of the directions or engage in any other relevant communication. ("Where are the pants?" "I finished cleaning the mirror," etc.) You could even make one of them the junior floor manager and have him or her direct some of the setting up. (You're the senior floor manager, of course.)

When you are satisfied with the condition of the store, announce in a grand, bold voice, "The store is now open for business."

Remember that the imaginary racks and tables of clothing form parallel rows and aisles leading up to their respective pictures on the chalkboard. Shoppers can stand in the imaginary aisles as they browse through the imaginary merchandise.

MORE ACTION

Assign two or three students to be sales clerks and bring them into the Arena. One should stand near the sales counter. The other(s) can wander around waiting to be helpful.

Bring four student shoppers to the front of the room. You may want to carry out the activity separately for girls, then boys, or you may want groups of mixed gender—whatever seems most natural for your students. Let's start with girls.

Making a selection

➤ (to all four girls) Go outside the store. (Gesture them out the classroom door into the hall.)
Now, come into the store. (Gesture them back in.)
(to one of the clerks) Smile at the shoppers.
Say, "May I help you?"
(to one of the shoppers) Say, "Yes, I want to buy a blouse."
(to the clerk) Say, "This way."
Guide the shoppers to the blouse rack. (She does.)
(to the shopper) Pick up a blouse and look at it.
Say "No," and put it back.
Pick up another blouse.
Now pick up a pink L card from the blouse stack.

The blouse is imaginary. The card is real but functions only as a symbol for size and color. It also helps students learn size and color words.

➤ Hold up the pink card for everyone to see.
Say to your friends, "I like this blouse. It's pink."
Go into the changing room.
Close the curtain!
Put on the blouse.
Come out of the changing room.
Look in the mirror.
(to one of the friends) Say, "That blouse is too large." (She says it.)
(to the shopper) Say to the clerk, "Do you have a smaller one?"
(to the clerk) Bring her a small, pink blouse.

Guide the clerk to lifting an imaginary blouse off the rack and taking a pink S card from the blouse section of the chalkboard.

➤ (to the clerk) Say, "Here. Try this one."
Give her the small pink blouse.
(to the shopper) Go back into the changing room.
Close the curtain!
Put on the blouse.
Come out of the changing room.
Look in the mirror.
(to another friend) Say, "That blouse is too small." (She says it.)
(to the clerk) Bring her a medium pink blouse.

Guide the clerk to lifting another imaginary blouse off the rack and taking a pink M card from the blouse section of the chalkboard.

➤ (to the clerk) Say, "Here, try this one."
Give her the medium pink blouse.
(to the shopper) Go back into the changing room.
Close the curtain!
Put on the blouse.
Come out of the changing room.
Look in the mirror.
Smile.
Say, "This one is jusssssst right!"
(to another of the friends) Say, "I like green better than pink. Try a green one." (She says it.)

And so on. As you can see, this activity could go on forever. If the students are learning and having fun, keep it going. When they tire of it, cut it off or bring in variations. You don't need a tedious Goldilocks saga for every item of apparel. You should, however, have the shoppers complete the purchase. And you should have other groups of shoppers follow the process as well, repeating the same commands and guiding them through the same movements and words so that the language sinks in.

Completing the purchase
➤ (to the shopper) Take the blouse to the sales counter.
(to the clerk at the sales counter) Say, "Will that be cash or charge?" (Demonstrate cash and charge, showing money and a credit card.)
(to the shopper) Say, "Credit."

Give the clerk your credit card.
(to the clerk) Swipe the card.
Give the shopper the sales slip.
(to the shopper) Sign the sales slip.
(to the clerk) Say, "Thank you."
Smile.
Give the shopper back her credit card.
(to the four shoppers) Go out of the store. (They go through the classroom door and into the hallway.)

Follow the same patterns with other groups of shoppers and other articles of clothing as long as the activity holds student interest.

To the extent that students are ready to speak, encourage them to add commands and responses themselves. The shopper's friends, for example, might express their feelings about the blouse (or whatever) and their suggestions about what to try next on their own, without your explicit command to say something. Or the clerks could play a more independent role, showing the shoppers the merchandise and saying things like "very nice material," or "very nice color," with less of your direct guidance.

FOLLOW-UP

With the students back in their seats, have them point to items or use other gestures as you direct.

Point to the rack of boys' shirts.
Point to the rack of girls' blouses.
Point the baseball hats.
Show me small. (Model how they should hold their hands near one another.)
Show me medium. (Model how they should hold their hands about a foot apart.)
Show me large. (Model how they should stretch their arms apart as far as they can.)
Etc.

Depending on how much students are ready to say, pick up colored cards from their place on the chalk tray and ask questions.
What color is this? ("Yellow")
What color and size is this? ("Yellow and large")
What is this? ("It's a large yellow boy's shirt.")

3.3 Sports on Television

For this activity the Arena is a television screen. The television receives only sports channels.

- Channel 1: Baseball
- Channel 2: Soccer
- Channel 3: Tennis
- Channel 4: Basketball
- Channel 5: Olympic Swimming

PREPARATION

First, make a large (8.5 x 11 in. or 22 x 28 cm or so) card for each of these channels, with a different color for each. Label the cards in big letters (for example, Channel 1: Baseball). Also, put the same labels in big letters on the chalkboard and draw a box around each. Line the boxes up horizontally.

Before you begin the activity, give students a copy of the Sports on Television reproducible page for their notebooks, and ask them to draw larger versions of the labeled pictures for posting so that everyone can see them from anywhere in the room. The pictures will contain many of the objects and much of the vocabulary associated with the scenario. The posted pictures will provide visual cues for the student as the scenario goes along.

Select a student to operate the remote and give him the five channel cards. Demonstrate his task, which will be to change to a channel by holding up the card and saying what the card says. For example, "Channel 3, Tennis!" Initially, he should respond only to your commands. Eventually, the students may want to change the channel on their own. Let it happen, but find the right balance between fun and chaos.

You, as teacher, can also change the channel by tapping the corresponding box on the chalkboard and calling out the channel and sport.

MORE ACTION

🠒 (to student with remote) Turn to Channel 1. (He does.)
Say, "Channel 1, baseball." (He does.)

Bring three students to the front of the room and position them at the plate, on the pitcher's mound, and in the outfield.

➤ (to the batter) Stand here.
Take the bat. (Give him the bat.)
Swing it a couple of times.
(to the pitcher) Stand here.
Hold the ball. (Give her the ball.)
(to the outfielder) Stand here.
Put your glove on. (Show him how.)

Now, let the game begin.

➤ (to the pitcher) Pitch the ball to the batter. (Pitcher pitches.)
(to the batter) Swing at the ball. (He swings.)

You, the teacher, are the umpire (as well as the referees, chair umpire, and judges for the other sports). You call balls, strikes, hits, and outs. After this pitch, call, "Strike one!"

➤ (to the pitcher) Pitch the ball again. (Pitcher pitches.)
(to the batter) Swing the bat again. (He swings again.)

This time say, "It's a high, fly ball," and follow it with your eyes way up in the air, arcing around and down toward the outfielder.

➤ (to the outfielder) Catch the ball. (Outfielder catches the ball.)
(to the batter) You're out! Go back to the dugout. (Gesture him back to his seat.)
(to another student) Next batter, come to the plate. (Gesture the student to come up to the plate.)
(to the new batter) You forgot your bat. Go back and get a bat. (Student goes back, picks up an imaginary bat, and returns to the plate.)
(to the pitcher) Pitch the ball.

She pitches. You might need to show her how to wind up. The more exaggerated some of these imaginary motions are, the better.

➤ (to the batter) Swing at the pitch. (Batter swings.)

Announce, "It's a ground ball up the middle," and track the ball with your eyes, showing everyone where it is.

➤ (to the outfielder) Catch the ball.
(to the batter) Run to first base. (Gesture him there.)
(to the outfielder) Throw the ball to the pitcher. (He does.)

Announce, "The runner is safe on first. Next batter!" Bring up another student.

- (to the next batter) Come to the plate, and remember your bat.
  Show me your bat. (She does. Say, "Good!")
  (To the pitcher) Wind up.
  Pitch to the batter.
  (to the batter) Swing at the ball. (Batter swings).

Announce, "It's a long, fly ball, way up in the air!" (Gesture the flight path. This baby's headed out of the park!) "That ball is going, going . . ."

- (to student with remote) Change to Channel 3.

You'll have to show him how to do this. He should click his imaginary remote and hold up his Channel 3: Tennis card.

- Say, "Channel 3, tennis."
  (to all the baseball players) Go back to your seats. The channel has changed. (Get them back to their seats quickly.)

Select two other students to play tennis and bring them to the front of the room, facing each other at opposite ends of the imaginary net.

- (to the tennis players) Show me your racquets.
  (to tennis player 1) Show me the ball. (Player should hold up the imaginary ball.)
  (to tennis player 1) Serve the ball. (You may need to demonstrate.)
  (to tennis player 2) Return the ball with a forehand. (Demonstrate.)
  (to tennis player 1) Hit the ball with a backhand. (Demonstrate.)
  (to both players) Keep hitting the ball back and forth.

As they hit, turn your head back and forth, back and forth, back and forth. Eventually, watch the ball go over player 2's head and call "Out!"

- (to tennis player 1) Serve the ball again.
  (to tennis player 2) Return the ball with a backhand.
  (to tennis player 1) Hit the ball with a forehand.
  (to tennis player 2) Run to the net.

Hit a drop shot. (Show what a drop shot is.)
(to tennis player 1) Run to the net.
Hit a passing shot. (Watch the ball go past player 2 for a winner.)

Continue the match with as much variation and detail as you want, or switch to another channel. As the activity develops, you may wish to have the same students always playing the same sport, with no crossover. That way when the student with the remote or you switch channels, the players of that sport will have to quickly take their positions on the field, court, or pool.

The amount of terminology that you bring in for each sport should depend on how much your students already know and how much they can absorb. Chances are good that they already know some, and that they'll be motivated to pick up more. Many terms cross over from one sport to another (ball, court, lines, referee, etc.) while others are specific to some sports (bat, racquet, basket, pool, etc.) This crossing over could confuse your students or it could solidify their understanding as they realize how common terms vary across different sports. It is likely that the same is true for their native language. Be alert to how they are responding to these terms, and either help them where they're shaky or take advantage of what they understand and run with it.

One more sport. After this you can go on to more channel changing and other sports. You can also come back to this activity in subsequent weeks or months whenever the students want to play a game instead of learning English.

ACTION CONTINUED

➤ (to student with remote) Change to Channel 5.
Say, "Channel 5, swimming."

Bring three groups of four students each into the Arena. They should form three lines, along the left side of the Arena and should be facing the right side, like relay swimmers.

You say, "On your mark!" Then—

➤ (to the first person in each row) Step to the edge of the pool.

You say, "Set!"

➤ (To the first person in each row) Bend your knees.
Put your arms out, ready to dive in the pool.

You say, "Go!"

~~ (to the first person in each row) Dive in the pool. (They step forward, making it look as much like a dive as they can in the Arena.)
Swim across the pool. (Their arms should flail and splash as they plow through the water to the opposite side. Keep them from just walking fast.)
(when they get to the other side) Touch the side.
Turn.
Swim back to the first side.
Tag the next person in line.
(to the second person in each row) Dive in the pool.
Swim across to the other side.
(to the first person in each row) Climb out of the pool.
Dry yourself off with a towel.
(to the current swimmers, when they reach the side) Touch the side.
Turn.
Swim back to the first side.
Etc.

You can keep it going to the end of the race, or you can have the student with the remote switch channels before the race ends. As with other activities, let the students lead in whatever ways will keep them engaged and keep the flow of language and action going.

REVIEW

As with nearly all the Arena activities, you can review all of the language posted on the wall by pointing to a labeled picture and having the students say the word or by saying the word and having the students point to the labeled picture. As you carry out this kind of review, both you and the students will be able to gauge how much they've learned and what they missed.

3.4 The Neighborhood

The Arena for this activity is a neighborhood, including a house with a front porch and steps leading down to the sidewalk and the street. Along the sidewalk are a tree, a trash barrel, and a fire hydrant (all imaginary, of course). The student desks that you have shoved back are across the street from the house, so students seated in them face the front steps and porch. A couple of student desks could be placed in the front of the classroom, to serve as the steps that students will sit on for much of the activity.

PREPARATION

Before launching the activity, give students a copy of the neighborhood reproducible page for their notebooks, and ask them to draw larger versions of the labeled pictures for posting so that everyone can see them from anywhere in the room. The pictures will contain many of the objects and much of the vocabulary associated with the scenario. The posted pictures will provide visual cues for the student as the scenario goes along.

ACTION

Begin by bringing two or three students into the Arena and sitting them on the front steps. Position another student to the side of the Arena by the classroom door. He will be the driver of a car. (He is actually way down the street, though still in the Arena.)

➤ (to the driver) Open your car door. (He does.)
   Get into the car.
   Fasten your seat belt.
   Start the engine.
   Drive slowly down the street. (across the Arena, in front of the steps)
   (when he arrives directly in front of the steps) Stop the car.
   Honk the horn.
   Say, "Beep-beep."
   Wave to your friends on the steps.
   Say, "Good morning, neighbors!"
   (to the step-sitters) Say, "Good morning, (name)!"
   (to the driver) Say, "Nice day, isn't it?"
   (to the step-sitters) Say, "Yes, it is!"
   (to the driver) Say, "See you later."
   Drive the rest of the way down the street.

When the driver is gone, send him back to his seat and bring up another student to be a driver. Position him down the street (to the side of the Arena) like the first driver. You may want to have a real gum wrapper or paper wad or something.
➤ (to the new driver) Get into your car.
   Drive slowly down the street.
   (when he is in front of the steps) Throw your gum wrapper out the window. (He does.)

Drive the rest of the way down the street.
(to the step-sitters) Stand up.
Make angry faces.
Say, "Oh, no!"
Run down the steps.
Shake your fists at the car.
(to one step-sitter)
Pick up the gum wrapper.
Throw it in the trash barrel.
(to both step-sitters) Go back to the steps.
Sit down.

Send driver 2 back to his seat, and position another student at the end of the street in the same place the drivers started from. This student will have an imaginary dog on a leash.

(to the dog walker) Put the leash on your dog.
Pet the dog.
Say to the dog, "Good dog!"
Say to the dog, "Let's go for a walk."
Hold the leash.
Start walking down the street. (not too far)
Stop.
Turn around.
Pull hard on the leash.
Say, "Come on, Elvis! Let's go!"
Turn forward again.
Continue walking.
(when the dog walker gets in front of the steps) Stop.
Wave to your neighbors.
Say, "Good morning!"
(to the step-sitters) Wave back.
Say, "Good morning to you!"
(to the dog-walker) Say, "Nice day, isn't it?"
(to the step-sitters) Say, "Yes, it is!"
(to one step-sitter) Say, "What is your dog's name?"
(to the dog-walker) Say, "His name is Elvis."
(to the other step-sitter) Say, "Uh... what is Elvis doing?"
(to the dog-walker) Look down at Elvis.
Put your hand on your forehead. (Demonstrate, if you need to.)
Shout, "Oh, no! Bad dog, Elvis."
Take out your dustpan and broom.

Sweep Elvis's mess into your dustpan.

Dump the dustpan into the trash barrel.

Say to the step-sitters, "Sorry!"

(to the step-sitters) Say, "That's OK!"

(to the dog-walker) Look at the tree. (Show him where the tree is.)

Say, "This tree needs water."

Continue walking Elvis to the end of the street.

(to the step-sitters) Stand up.

Go to the tree.

Look closely at the tree.

Look at each other.

Say, "He's right!"

(to one step-sitter) Say, "Go get the watering can."

(to the other step-sitter) Go back to the steps.

Pick up the watering can.

Go back to the tree.

Water the tree.

(to both step-sitters) Go to the trash barrel.

Look in the trash barrel.

Hold your nose.

Look at each other.

Say, "P–U."

Go back to the steps.

Sit down.

You can repeat the same scenarios with different students, or you can invent some new ones yourself. As with most other Arena activities, you can do this one, then come back to it weeks later with variations.

FOLLOW UP

Review, reinforcement, and assessment

Review the language posted on the wall by pointing to a labeled picture and having the students say the word or by saying the word and having the students point to the labeled picture. As you carry out this kind of review, both you and the students will be able to gauge how much they've learned and what they missed.

Language elements

Register: polite conversation	3.4
Adjectives/adverbs	
colors	3.2
sizes	3.2
Location words	3.1
Verbs associated with sports	3.3
Vocabulary	
living room furniture	3.1
clothing	3.2
department store features	3.2
sports and sports equipment	3.3
neighborhood fixtures	3.4

Story Telling

As teachers know, a well-told tale weaves magic with a class. It binds students together through their shared journey, expanding each and enriching all amid their developing classroom culture. It becomes a common resource, nurturing them outward toward new knowledge and skills in many fields and inward toward deeper human understandings.

This chapter will approach learning through one story that has hundreds of variations across dozens of cultures, Cinderella. Through centuries, the story has appealed to children, acknowledging their fears that the world is not always safe while also reassuring them that there are forces that can protect them. From wherever your students are, the activities suggested in this chapter will carry them more deeply into the English language as well as into many other areas of knowledge, skill, and understanding.

The activities include three journeys through a Cinderella tale and extensive follow-up for each. The first is an Arena-style pantomime, in which you give commands to your students and they perform the actions wordlessly. The second is a combination of narration, which you provide, and drama, which the students provide. In the third, you (or any students who are ready) read an illustrated storybook version to the class and show them the pictures.

Some follow-up strategies are included with each of the three versions of the story. But since many worthwhile approaches apply to any or all of the versions, an extensive list of suggestions appears separately in a fourth section. These varied approaches lead your students not only more fully into language but also into learning that will support them in other classes.

You should be sure that you and your students are familiar with the Arena concept and procedures from Chapter 3 before tackling this chapter.

You should also proceed with each version of the story in the order in which it appears here: pantomime, then drama-narration, then storybook reading. The progression will gradually increase the language challenges for your students while also building an increasingly supportive scaffold to help them rise to those challenges.

The approach presented here—multiple journeys through variations of the same story—capitalizes on something teachers know but do not always apply: The more students know about anything, the more they are able to learn. The approach also presents opportunities for learning at a variety of levels. Because the story is so widely known across cultures, many children began to build their scaffold before they came to your class, and the progressive nature of the activities will strengthen that scaffold. Your focus on the story is likely to affirm a bit of their past to children recently arrived on the North American mainland. Look for signs of recognition and build on them when they appear.

Finally, before you begin the activities in this chapter, go to your friendly neighborhood library and take out an armload of Cinderella storybooks with pictures from among the many enchanting options you will find. Each story is unique, yet each has much in common with the others, and all are powerful and compelling.

Hide these books in a cupboard until after you have finished the first activity—the pantomime. For that activity—if at all possible—do not tell the students what the story is or the names of any characters. Just carry out the pantomime and watch your students to see whether and when recognition dawns. It will.

Then, after eliciting all that you can about what they know of the story and before going on to the second activity, scatter the library books around the room and give students time to explore.

In the 1980s, a number of ESOL teachers in Rochester, New York, read and discussed many different Cinderella stories with their students, whose experience in English ranged from a few months to a few years. The teachers reported widespread recognition and spontaneous responses from their students, who showed an almost urgent need to talk and share. If your class shows a similar inclination, let it flow.

4.1 Cinderella Pantomime

PREPARATION

In this activity, the students present the story of Cinderella through pantomime. They use the imaginary classroom Arena as a stage (see

Chapter 3), and they follow your commands. Students not involved in the acting (or not on stage at a particular time) stay in their seats and form the audience.

Once established as part of the class culture, Cinderella will lead to various subsequent activities and rich language learning. The initial approach through pantomime will work no matter how much or how little English your students know.

For this first encounter, the language to be understood focuses on words that convey mood, emotion, looks, or components of character: *smile, cry, frown, laugh* (verbs); *happy, sad, angry, excited, afraid, selfish, wicked,* (adjectives). Vocabulary will also include common features of the scene: *broom, fireplace, mirror, gown, magic wand,* and the verb *sweep.* And almost without explicit attention, students will learn the verb commands through which you guide the action. Copy the Cinderella pantomime reproducible page for each of your students, and have them draw larger labeled images for posting around the room.

Do not tell the actors (or anyone in the class) who they are at the beginning (Cinderella, stepmother, stepsisters, prince, etc.). That way, you can discover students' prior knowledge of the story. If students recognize the story from their own cultures, elicit whatever they can tell you. The activity is presented with the assumption that you have chosen not to give them names right away.

PERFORMANCE

Cast
Cinderella
Stepmother
Stepsister 1
Stepsister 2
Fairy Godmother
Prince
Dancers (4 or so)

Props
a rolled-up sheet of paper to serve as a proclamation
a ruler to serve as a magic wand
a paper crown from a fast-food restaurant or party supply store

Identify the actors ahead of time, and seat them so they can easily get in and out of their chairs. To avoid using names, indicate whom you are giving commands to through gestures.

Scene 1

 (to Cinderella) Sit here, by the fireplace.

Look sad.

(to stepmother and stepsisters) Bustle into the room.

Look at her. (Meaning Cinderella, but don't say the name.)

Look angry.

Point to the broom.

Point to her. (Cinderella)

Point to the broom again, angrily.

Put your hands on your hips.

(to Cinderella) Stand up.

Look sad.

Take the broom.

Slowly, sadly, begin sweeping the floor.

(after a while, to everyone) Stop.

Stand still.

Having everyone stop and stand still in a silent tableau will indicate the end of each scene and the passing of time. Whenever there is a door in a scene, use the classroom door.

Scene 2

 (to Cinderella) Begin sweeping the floor again.

(You, as teacher, knock on the door.)

(to stepmother) Walk to the door.

Open the door.

Take this proclamation. (Give rolled-up sheet of paper to her.)

Read the proclamation.

Look happy and excited.

Jump up and down.

Hold the proclamation up.

Show it to the others.

(to stepsisters) Gather close to her. (the stepmother)

(to Cinderella) Stand behind them. (the stepsisters)

(to the stepsisters) Read the proclamation.

Jump up and down.

Clap your hands.

Look excited.

Look happy.

Keep looking happy.

(to Cinderella) Smile.

Clap your hands.

Look happy.

(to the stepsisters) Stand still.

Frown at her. (Cinderella)

Look angry.

(to Cinderella) Stand still.

Stop smiling.

(to the stepsisters) Point to the fireplace.

Point to her. (Cinderella)

Point to the fireplace again.

(to Cinderella) Look sad.

Sit down by the fireplace.

(to everyone) Stand still.

Pause briefly to indicate time passing. Then walk quietly to the light switch. Turn the lights off, then pause. Turn them on, and pause again. Repeat. (Or if you can find a better way to indicate the passing of day and night, do it.)

Scene 3

 (to the stepsisters) Look in the mirror.

Make ugly faces.

(to stepsister 1) Put on lipstick, hard!

(to stepsister 2) Brush your hair, hard!

(to stepsister 1) Brush your hair, hard!

(to stepsister 2) Put on lipstick, hard!

(to both stepsisters) Pinch your faces, hard!

(to stepmother) Walk around the girls.

Smile.

(to Cinderella) Walk near the girls.

Smile.

(to stepmother and stepsisters) Look at her. (Cinderella)

Frown at her.

Look angry.

(to Cinderella) Stop smiling.

(to stepmother and stepsisters) Point to the fireplace.

Put your hands on your hips.

(to Cinderella) Look sad.

Sit down by the fireplace.

(to stepmother and stepsisters) Put on long gowns.

Smile at each other.

(to stepsister 1) Look at yourself in the mirror.

Smile.

(to stepsister 2) Push in front of her (stepsister 1)

Look at yourself in the mirror.

Smile.

(to stepsister 1) Push in front of her (stepsister 2)

Smile.

(to stepmother) Take girls by the hand.

Lead them out of the room. (Have them go back to their seats.)

(to Cinderella, still sitting) Look very sad.

Cry.

Wipe your eyes.

Stand still.

Scene 4

(to Fairy Godmother) Come into the room. (She should be carrying the ruler.)

(to Cinderella) Look at her.

Look surprised.

Look afraid.

(to Fairy Godmother)

Smile at her. (Cinderella)

Pat her head gently.

Smile at her.

Point to her.

Point to the door.

(to Cinderella) Stand up.

Point to yourself.

Indicate the rags you're wearing as clothing.

Shake your head no.

(to Fairy Godmother) Smile.

Touch her clothing with your magic wand.

Stand back.

(to Cinderella) Open your mouth wide.

Look surprised.

Look at the beautiful gown.

Look in the mirror.

Touch the gown.

Look at her. (Fairy Godmother)

(to Fairy Godmother) Gesture toward the door.

(to Cinderella) Gesture toward yourself.

Look surprised.

Look questioning.

(to Fairy Godmother) Nod yes.

Take her by the hand.

Lead her to the door.

Stop.

Point to the clock.

Shake a finger at her. (Cinderella)

Lead her out the door.
(End of scene 4)

For scene 5, bring your dancers on stage. Start them dancing around. They don't have to dance with each other (which may be unthinkable for certain age groups), but they should glide around the room and turn gracefully. You could hum a few bars of the "Merry Widow Waltz," the "Blue Danube," or something to get them started. They should smile as they dance, happy subjects of a happy kingdom. They should be dancing as the scene opens.

Scene 5

(to stepmother and stepsisters) Appear in the doorway.
Look at the dancers.
Smile a selfish smile.
Come on to the dance floor.
Dance clumsily.
Bump into other dancers.
(to the prince, who is wearing a paper crown) Stand in the doorway.
(to all dancers) Stop dancing.
Bow to the prince.
(to the prince) Wave your hand in a circle to tell them to keep dancing.
(to the dancers) Dance again. (Give them a few more bars of "The Merry Widow Waltz," if they need it.)
(to the stepsisters) Go up to him. (the prince)
Grab his sleeves.
Pull him to the center of the dance floor.
Keep pulling him to the opposite side. (opposite the door)
Dance around him clumsily.
Bump into him.
Step on his foot.
(to the prince) Say, "Ouch!" (the only word in the pantomime)
Look at the wicked girls. (the stepsisters)
Look afraid.
(to Cinderella) Stand in the doorway.
(to the prince) Look at the girl in the doorway.
Go over to her.
Bow to her.
Take her hand.
Lead her to the center of the dance floor.
Dance gently and smoothly with her.
(to stepmother and stepsisters) Look at the two dancers.

Look angry.

Make angry motions with your hands.

(to everyone) Stand still.

Scene 6

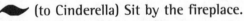 (to Cinderella, the prince, and the dancers) Everyone begin dancing again.

(to stepmother and stepsisters) Stand by the wall.

Look angry.

(to Cinderella) Look at the clock.

Put a hand over your mouth.

Look afraid.

Run toward the door.

Stumble.

Limp the rest of the way out the door.

(to the prince) Follow her.

Stop where she stumbled.

Pick up the glass slipper.

Go to the door.

Look out the door.

Look at the slipper in your hand.

Look out the door again.

(to everyone) Stand still.

Hold the tableau briefly, then send everyone back to their seats.
Bring Cinderella, the stepmother, and the stepsisters back on stage.

Scene 7

(to Cinderella) Sit by the fireplace.

(to stepmother and stepsisters) Look angry.

Pace back and forth across the room.

(to the prince) Appear in the doorway.

(to stepmother and stepsisters) See him in the doorway.

Smile your wicked, selfish smiles.

Clap your hands.

(to the prince) Hold up the glass slipper.

(to stepsister 1) Grab his sleeve.

Pull him into the room

Stick out your foot.

Point to it.

(to the prince) Try to put the slipper on her foot.

Shake your head no.

(to stepsister 2) Grab his sleeve.

Point to yourself.

Stick out your foot.

(to the prince) Try to put the slipper on her foot.

Shake your head no.

(to stepmother and stepsisters) Look angry.

(to the prince) See the girl sitting by the fireplace.

Hold the glass slipper toward her.

Start to walk toward her.

(to stepmother and stepsisters) Stand in front of him to block his way.

Shake your heads no.

(to the prince) Walk past them to the girl. (Cinderella)

Take her foot.

Put the slipper on it.

Take her hand.

Help her stand up.

Bow to her.

Walk her to the center of the stage.

(to the prince and Cinderella) Face the audience.

Smile.

Face each other.

Bow to each other.

Hold both hands.

(to everyone) Stand still.

(Curtain call)

 (to everyone) Come on the stage.

(to the dancers) Line up facing the audience.

Bow.

(to the fairy godmother) Come to the center of the stage.

Bow.

(to stepmother and stepsisters) Come to the center of the stage.

Bow.

(to Cinderella and the prince) Come to the center of the stage.

Bow.

(to everyone) Bow together.

FOLLOW-UP

Consolidating understanding

If some of your students recognize the story as "Cinderella," elicit from them what they know about the story. Be sure they understand who the characters were in the pantomime, and then encourage them to explore similarities and differences among them. See Section 4.4 for further suggestions in connection with this activity.

Confirming vocabulary

You can also confirm their learning of some of the language they encountered in the pantomime and assess that learning. Say words like *angry, sad,* and *happy,* and ask students to show the feeling on their faces. Or make the faces yourself, and ask them to say the word for the expression. Say a word with its picture on the wall (broom, mirror, etc.) and ask the students to point to the correct picture or to the location of the imaginary object in the Arena.

For the words that convey actions or feelings (e.g., smile, angry), you can help students sort the words by such categories as good and attractive on one hand and evil and unattractive on the other. Use the categories to reinforce and assess students' grasp of the meanings of the words.

Extending to writing

Try pairing the pantomime with appropriate writing tasks. For some students, simply copying a one-word command from the board may be sufficient. Others may be able to write phrases or full sentences. Advanced students could add stage directions.

4.2 Drama-Narration

PREPARATION

"Billy Beg and His Bull" is an Irish version of the Cinderella story. In this story, unlike most others, the central character is a boy. The script for this activity, set forth on the reproducible pages, blends narration, dramatic dialogue, and lots of action.

The narration is intended to be read aloud by you, the teacher, with student-actors playing assigned roles and reading their assigned lines as dramatic dialogue. Your classroom Arena (see Chapter 3) is the stage, with nonacting students serving as the audience. Some few stage directions for the student-actors appear parenthetically at the beginning of the play, but most, and very soon all, are embedded in the narrative itself. Don't miss them! Wherever a stage direction appears, be sure your student-actors carry it out, preferably in broad, exaggerated strokes. Guide them in doing so even if you have to interpret or supplement the narration, and leave plenty of time for the action to take place even if you have to pause in the middle of a sentence.

Much of the narration, in its choice of word and detail, its beauty, its repetition of phrases, and its boundless exaggeration, carries all the bounce and swagger of poetic language. As such, some of it will be a

        0-7682-3072-1   *Ready, Set, Speak*

stretch for students. That's why the actions are important. They will fill in the gaps, and the magic of the story will fill in the rest.

PERFORMANCE

Copy enough scripts for yourself and your actors from the reproducible pages and begin your journeys.

FOLLOW-UP

Rehearsals

Because the students (actors and audience) will need to process words from the script and actions from your narration, the first times through this play will feel rough. So it is with any play. That's why they have rehearsals. But even stumbling through a scene a couple of times brings learning—what to say, how to move, etc. Don't allow yourself or your students to become discouraged—just play scenes over a few times to smooth them out. Repetition will enhance students' learning and bolster their confidence as they find themselves suddenly doing something that was hard and awkward a few moments earlier. Judge how much rehearsal you need, then at some point run through the whole play, remaining stumbles and all.

Vocabulary

The play is rich in vocabulary, especially nouns that name things and lively action verbs. Here are a couple of activities for reinforcing, reviewing, and assessing the vocabulary of the play.

Select the nouns from a list such as the following: *bull, blood, forest, napkin, hills, rocks, stick, sword, herd-boy, cows, donkeys, goats, pasture, giant, fire, armpits, brook, shoulders, dozen, neck(s), arena* (stadium-type), *princess, champion, coach (or carriage), wheelbarrow, well* (for water). Obtain pictures of each of these nouns and post them around the room. Write the nouns themselves on 3 x 5 in. (8 x 13 cm) sticky notes and put them on a desk in the middle of the Arena.

One at a time, students come to the front, take a sticky note, read it aloud, and paste it on the corresponding picture. Continue this procedure until all pictures are tagged.

Then have a big old ugly mean giant (you) remove all the sticky notes while bellowing something terrifying, like "Fee! Fie! Foe! Fum! I'm gonna steal your tags, by gum!"

Place the notes in odd spots around the room—on a window, on the chalkboard, on a student's nose, etc. When you're finished, laugh a roaring, evil laugh and tell the students that you'll bet them that they can't get all the sticky notes back on the proper pictures in less than two minutes.

Then stand back.

Before you start removing the notes, hang a big sign saying "Giant" around your neck. When you make the bet, you can tell the students that if they succeed, you'll wear the sign clothes-pinned to your nose for ten minutes. Motivation, you know.

Select your verbs from a list such as the following: *kill, jump(ed), leap(ed), gallop, ride/rode, shake/shook, spit/spitting (fire), wave, wring/wrung (her hands)*. Write each verb (and a sentence containing it from the play, for context) on a 4 x 6 in. (10 x 15 cm) card, and put all the cards on a desk in the center of the Arena.

Ask students—one at a time—to come up, pick a card, not read it aloud, but act out the action it expresses. Examples: Gallop—gallop around the room a couple of times as though riding a horse (or bull); wave (the stick in the air three times); kill (the dragon). The rest of the class should try to figure out the word being demonstrated and raise their hands when they know. Tell them not to shout out the answer, in order to give more students time to come up with the answer. When you have enough hands in the air, ask the performing student to call on someone and then to say if the answer is right or not.

4.3 Picture Book Story Reading

PREPARATION

On your preparatory trip to the library, you found armloads of Cinderella stories that you scattered around the classroom. They include stories about Yeh-Shen in ancient China, Rhodopis in ancient Egypt, and Settareh, the beautiful, lonely Cinderella of old Persia. You picked up some Russian tales. In some of these, our heroine doesn't even have a name, while in others, from many different times and places in Russia, she is Vasilisa: Vassilisa the Wise, Vasilissa the Beautiful, or Vasilisa the Brave, whom Baba Yaga, the fearsome witch with iron teeth, hopes to eat for dinner. You found Cinderellas from the Philippines to Western Europe, from Vietnam to the Spanish-American Southwest, and from Iceland to almost everywhere in Africa. You brought in the Algonquin Indians' Rough-Face Girl on the shores of Lake Ontario. You were delighted to find a rap version, Cinder-Elly, where the prince is a basketball player in a New York City high school and where Cinder-Elly loses a glass sneaker as she runs out of the gym too late and finds that her bike has turned back into a garbage can.

For this activity, ask your students for suggestions and select one of these beautifully written and illustrated stories. And then, perhaps, another, and another, and another.

The Reading

Begin the activity by reading your storybook to your students, showing them the pictures and providing explanation as you go along. Just listening to the story and looking at the pictures will be a rich learning activity for them. Because of their experience with the pantomime and dramatic narrative, each new trip through a Cinderella tale will feel increasingly familiar.

Journey through the story again, having students share in the reading aloud and showing of pictures.

Pantomime

Divide the class into small groups, and have each group take a scene and generate a pantomime of the scene. They can then generate commands for the actions in their scene and then perform the scene, with one student giving the commands and the others carrying them out.

Writing dialogue

In small groups, students could turn the narrative prose of their assigned scenes into dialogue and then perform their scene for the class.

Comparing versions

Students can of course discuss their insights to the story, comparing its elements with those from the other stories they've worked with and know. Graphic organizers, particularly Venn diagrams, work well to help students organize their thoughts.

Confirming vocabulary

Small groups of students could make lists of words that they remember from the story or that they think are important. They could put the words in two columns on newsprint: words they know and words they want to learn. The newsprint goes up on the walls, and each group presents its list for class comment.

Illustrating scenes

Groups of students could draw and label components of a scene from the story on newsprint and present their work to the rest of the class. For an additional challenge, students can jumble the scenes together and reassemble them in sequence.

4.4 More Follow-Up Strategies

Following each of your journeys through Cinderella, you can choose to guide your students' learning in many different directions and at many different levels. The approaches here will generally provide effective follow-up for any of the story formats.

REPLAYS

Reiteration sharpens understanding. (Replays work best for the pantomime or drama-narration.) The power of listening to, performing, reading, and writing multiple versions of the same story has to be experienced. It reminds us that the more background students have, the more they are able to learn. It also reminds us of the importance of learning styles and multiple intelligences. How far you take your students in any of these directions depends on your sense of what they can do, what they want to do, what they'd better do, and what resources they bring to the party.

Instant replays

Simply repeat the presentation as originally done or with minor variations, such as having new students play the parts or having students who already played the parts read the commands or narration.

Different small groups could act out different segments. As long as it doesn't become a drag, the more students replay the actions, the deeper the stories will sink into their bones and muscles and hearts and brains, and the stronger their scaffolds for further learning.

In an activity reminiscent of an Arena activity, set up a different area of the room for each of the scenes of the presentation. A small group in each area should prepare the scene, rehearsing it until it is rapid and natural. Then, darken the room as best you can, and provide a few flashlights to students who become the lighting crew. Their job is to focus the beams on the appropriate scene in the proper order. When the lights are shined on a given scene, the small group of students performs.

More elaborate replay

Depending on the skill of your students and the time you want to put into this activity, consider a full-fledged dramatic production held in the school auditorium for a select and appreciative audience. Perhaps each student in your class is allowed to invite five friends or family members. Members of each scene place themselves on a darkened stage, assuming the pose that they want to show at the moment the lights are shined on them. Then, as the lighting moves to the next scene, they hold their last positions until they are sure that their scene is completed.

Genre transformation

Send students back through the story itself by having them transform it from pantomime to drama, drama to narrative, story to summary, etc., leading to a new product and perhaps a new performance. Again, you can break a version into pieces and have small groups work with each piece. The pantomime, for example, can be divided into scenes and doled out to groups whose task will be to translate the scene into dialogue (or narration), assign themselves roles, and perform their scene for the class. Or they could transform the drama-narration or storybook version into a pantomime. Think of how much language they will experience in both the process and the product!

EXPLICIT LANGUAGE LEARNING

Reiterate and review the language elements of the story: vocabulary, word order, command verbs (where they occur), idiomatic phrasing, sentences, etc.

Illustrating language

One approach is to have small groups draw and label pictures related to the story on newsprint, including key scenes, details, and objects. Each group would then post their work and describe it to the class. Alternatively, a group could draw pictures, point to a picture, and have the rest of the class say the word.

Creating categories

With the class, create categories for learning the words. Together with students, develop a list of words that apply to Cinderella, to the stepmother, to the sisters, the prince, and the fairy godmother. As a review activity later on, take the same words and categorize them differently: physical appearance, personality, positive words, negative words, etc.

SUPPORTING STUDY IN OTHER CLASSES

Strengthen your students' present or eventual work in any of their other classes.

Channeling familiarity

Students learn more easily when new information is linked to something that is already familiar. That's as true in science as it is in stories.

Did your students recognize Cinderella from their own past experiences? Channel their familiarity into discussions that compare and contrast the stories they know with the stories you lead them through. How do the parallel characters compare? How does magic work differently from one story to the other? If students have had prior encounters with the story, they will be eager to share them with their classmates. The most profound language learning results from just such a need to communicate.

Sequence and comprehension—reinforcing and assessing

Recognizing relationships is another way to help learning. One of the easiest relationships is simple sequencing. Sequence matters in history, mathematics, and science, as well as in stories.

Get a set of eight large cards on which you can write a few words in letters big enough to see across the room. On each, put key words that clearly come from a unique point in the version's sequence of events. Examples for the pantomime might include *Cinderella dances with prince; stepsisters brush hair; Cinderella tries on slipper*, etc. Examples for the drama-narration might include: *bull 1; champion jumps into well; bull 2* etc. Give each card to a different student and line them up randomly in the front of the room. Ask other students to put them in order.

Literary terms

Now that students have a deep understanding of the elements of story, expose them to some of the formal literary terms for concepts they have already discussed, such as *plot, character, setting, theme*, and more, depending on what they're ready for. As their discussions crystallize their sense of these concepts, they will be particularly ripe for learning the formal terms. For example:

- **Plot:** What is the sequence of events in the story? What is the problem, or conflict, that gives the story its direction? How does it end? Why is the ending right? Could the story have ended any other way?
- **Character:** What were the people in the story like? Why do you like some characters and dislike others? What different words can you use to describe each character? Did the characters seem real, or were they unlike any real people you know? Explain.

- **Setting:** Where did the story take place? What were the two settings? What did the settings tell you about the characters?
- **Theme:** What does the story say about life? What does it say about good and evil, selfishness and kindness, wealth and poverty, power and justice, etc.?

Writing original versions

For sufficiently advanced and/or creative students, encourage them to write their own original Cinderella story set in your classroom using classmates as characters. (You'll know how much they like you by whether they make you the wicked stepmother or the fairy godmother.) *Cinder-Elly* is a wonderful contemporary model, though you may find that, unless you intervene, your students' versions are all set at a basketball game.

Supporting social studies skills and knowledge

Assign students in groups of three or four to research how many countries have Cinderella stories and to prepare a chart listing countries, story names, Cinderella's name, etc. (They will be particularly motivated to find stories from their native lands.) Then, trot them off to your school's computer lab to do the research. (see resources). Once student charts are complete, hit up your social studies colleague for a big world map and put it on your wall. Students write the title and main character's name for each story on a big sticky note and put it on its corresponding country on the map for all to see. This kind of work with charts and maps will give your students a leg up in their social studies classes.

FURTHER REPETITIONS

After you and your students have discovered the power of repetition, you can extend beyond Cinderella. Enjoy researching Paul Bunyan, urban legends, Juan Bobo stories, and the wisdom of Nasruddin Hoja. Discovering these repeating stories and variations could become a life's work. Perhaps opportunities such as these are why we became teachers in the first place—to keep learning ourselves.

Language elements

Adjectives (emotion and character)	4.1
Vocabulary (Billy Beg story)	4.2
Literary terms	4.4

Resources

PRINT RESOURCES

Climo, Shirley. *The Persian Cinderella*. Art by Robert Florczak. New York: HarperCollins, 1999.
A retelling of the traditional Persian tale in which Settareh, neglected and abused by her stepmother and stepsisters, finds her life transformed with the help of a little blue jug. Climo has written other Cinderella stories as well.

Louie, Ai-Ling. *Yeh-Shen*. Illustrated by Ed Young. New York: Philomel Books, 1982.
This version of the Cinderella story, in which a young girl overcomes the wickedness of her stepsister and stepmother to become the bride of a prince, is based on ancient Chinese manuscripts written 1,000 years before the earliest European version.

Martin, Rafe. *The Rough-Face Girl*. Illustrated by David Shannon. New York: G.P. Putnam's Sons, 1992.
In this Algonquin Indian version of the Cinderella story, the Rough-Face Girl and her two beautiful but heartless sisters compete for the affections of the invisible being.

Mayer, Marianna. *Baba Yaga and Vasilisa the Brave*. Illustrated by K. Y. Craft. New York: William Morrow, 1994.
A retelling of the old Russian fairy tale in which beautiful Vasilisa uses the help of her doll to escape from the clutches of the witch Baba Yaga, who in turn sets in motion the events which lead to the once ill-treated girl's marrying the tsar.

Minters, Frances. *Cinder-Elly*. Illustrated by G. Brian Karas. New York: Penguin, 1994.
In this rap version, the overworked younger sister gets to go to a basketball game and meets a star player, Prince Charming.

Sherman, Josepha. *Vassilisa the Wise: A Tale of Medieval Russia*. Illustrated by Daniel San Souci. Harcourt Brace Jovanovich: San Diego, 1988.
A clever and beautiful woman uses her wits to get her husband out of Prince Vladimir's prison.

Winthrop, Elizabeth. *Vasilissa the Beautiful*. Illustrated by Alexander Koshkin. New York: HarperCollins, 1991.
A retelling of the old Russian fairy tale in which the beautiful Vasilissa uses the help of her doll to escape from the clutches of the witch Baba Yaga.

INTERNET RESOURCES

The de Grummond Children's Literature Collection

   The site http://avatar.lib.usm.edu provides, among other resources, a huge grid listing Cinderella stories by country, author, title, where you can find them, etc.

The Sur La Lune Fairy Tale Web site

   The site http://www.surlalunefairytales.com provides a long list of the stories across cultures. It also gives electronic text of the stories that are not copyrighted, and directs you to print versions of those that are copyrighted. It includes annotations and much more information.

The University of Pittsburgh Web site

   The site http://www.pitt.edu gives full electronic texts of a number of Cinderella stories.

0-7682-3072-1 *Ready, Set, Speak*

Games, Word Play, Songs, and Chants

Students sitting in classes disconsolately watch the clock as it ticks ever so slowly toward recess—a time to get up, stretch, move around, tell jokes, and play games. Why wait for the clock? Enlist their doleful yearning and latent energy in the service of advancing their acquisition of language.

Through games, word play, songs, and chants, the activities in this chapter not only get students out of their chairs but also rouse their spirits, spark their interest, tickle their funny bones, exercise their vocal cords, and strengthen their command over the sounds and senses of English.

5.1 Games for Small Spaces

From card games to board games to running-around and party games that children have played for years, games offer engaging opportunities for learning. Even the games for small spaces described below can, with a little adjustment, include some moving around.

CARD GAMES

Pairs or small groups of students can play card games that, with a little careful design and preparation, can be learning experiences as well as good practice. Most students will need to learn the rules, and they can do so by moving around. Start with a selection of paired picture cards from any inexpensive children's card game, such as Rummy or Go Fish. Soon you will purchase or create your own cards, tailored to the language that students are learning.

Snap

The goal of the basic Snap game is to wind up with all the cards. You accumulate cards by taking all the cards in the middle pile if the top two cards make a pair. To demonstrate the concept of pairs, start with any set of paired picture cards. Select eight cards (four matching sets), place them face down on your desk, and invite eight students to the front of the room. Depending on their language level, you may need to gently move them around in order to demonstrate your commands.

> (to all eight) Stand up.
> Walk to the front of the room.
> Take one card from my desk.
> Look at your card.
> Walk around, without talking.
> Look at other people's cards.
> When you find someone with the same card, stop.
> Congratulations! You have a pair. Show the class your pair of cards.
> Then put the cards back on my desk.
> Go back to your seat.
> Sit down.

Mix up the eight cards, put them back face down on your desk, and invite another group to perform the same routine. Or, if you prefer, create a whole-class challenge by putting all of the picture cards on your desk and inviting an equally large number of students to participate.

Now that students understand the concept of pairs, they need to know the sequence of play. Invite three students back to the front of the room and seat them around a table with you. At first, you are the dealer. Describe your actions as you proceed.

> I'm the dealer. I'm shuffling the cards. I'm dealing one card, face down, to each of us.
> And another.
> And another.
> (Continue until the deck is dealt.)
> (to the three students) Pick up your cards, but don't look at the

faces of the cards.

(to Student 1, on your left) Take the top card from your hand and put it face up on the table.

(to Student 2) Take the top card from your hand and put it on top of Student 1's card. (Leave a gap between the cards so all can still see the first card.)

(to all three students) Do those two cards make a pair?

(If they are a pair, yell "Snap!" and scoop up the two cards.)

I'm picking up the pair.

I'm putting it near me on the table.

or

(If the two cards are not a pair

(to Student 3) Take the top card from your hand and put it face up on top of the other cards.

Do the top two cards make a pair?

If the top two cards make a pair, the player takes the whole pile and puts it underneath the cards in his hand. Whoever spots a pair first can yell Snap and take the pile. Eventually players drop out when they play their last card. The winner is the only person with cards in his hand when everyone else has dropped out.

Make your own cards

Once the students have mastered the game and scoring with a simple game of Snap, it's time to prepare your own language cards. There's no limit to the number of words or parts of words that can make a pair. For beginning and intermediate students, make pairs of cards in which:

- a single word is duplicated, such as two cards for shirt, two for skirt, etc.
- one card is a word and the second is the corresponding picture
- there is a word and its synonym (e.g., house, home)
- there is a word and its opposite (e.g., happy, sad)

As students become more proficient in English, the cards can grow with them.

- prefix and root word pairs (e.g., un-, lock)
- compound word pairs (e.g., flowerpot)
- homonym word pairs or triplets (e.g., hoarse, horse; buy, by, bye)
- idiomatic phrases and their meanings (e.g., take a chair = sit down)
- specialized language that students will need in other classes (e.g., plus, +, and)

          0-7682-3072-1   *Ready, Set, Speak*

Reduce your own preparation time and offer students another learning experience by asking small groups to work together to make their own cards, following instructions that you and the class agree on and post on the board. Beginners, for example, can create duplicate sets of cards naming classroom objects. Point to an object, ask what it is, and either some student will respond or you tell them. Write the name of the object on the board, and then ask two students to copy the word onto two separate cards. Continue until you have a substantial deck of paired words for classroom objects.

As card games become a frequent and desirable activity in your class, it's likely that students will want to make their own decks to play at home with family and friends.

Concentration/Memory

Students can play this old familiar game as two competing individuals, as pairs competing against each other, or even as small teams.

To get students out of their chairs and moving around in a classroom-wide Concentration game, one group of students (initially with your help) tapes their student-created concentration cards in plain sight around the room. (The students who will play the game have to be elsewhere while the preparation is occurring.) For example, one of the paired cards, face down and stuck to a wall clock, says *clock*. Somewhere in the room, perhaps on a window, is a second face-down card that says *clock*. Of course, there are also other cards taped face down on that window. One card may be the winning *clock* card, but there's also a card that says *window* and maybe two other cards saying *wall* and *floor*.

Use a command sequence for setting up the cards. Assuming that the first card is indeed *clock*, say:

> (to two students) Pick up a pair of cards.
> Point to the clock. (One or both students point.)
> Take the roll of masking tape.
> Rip off a piece.
> Tape the first *clock* card face down on the clock.
> Tape the second *clock* card somewhere else.

Continue this series of commands with different word pairs and different student pairs until all the cards are placed. Now, invite the players back into the room.

> Who would like to start? Raise your hand if you want to be first.
> (You choose a student.)
> Turn over the first card. (You wave wildly around the room,

designating all the cards. She turns one over.)

Turn over a second card. (She does.)

Is it a pair? (Any member of the class can answer yes or no.)

(in the remote event that it's a pair) Good! Take down both cards and put them on the table.

or

(if it's not a pair) Too bad! Turn both cards back face down.

Make sure the tape sticks. (You help them rub the tape to make sure it's secure.)

Continue with volunteers until all the cards are paired and removed from the classroom. The game is finished, and the whole class has won. This whole-class introduction to Concentration is pleasant because it is not competitive. Anyone in the class can coach the volunteers, helping them remember where the cards are located. However, a careful study of human nature suggests that the students who placed the cards are unlikely to help, and some may even offer false advice.

This orientation to Concentration, described for beginners, is useful to explain to all levels of students how the game is played. Now take the same cards, place them face down on a table, and begin the traditional Concentration card game.

If you have a heterogeneous class with some students who do not yet know enough English to fully participate in a complicated matching game, designate these beginners as "turners." In this case, more advanced students aren't allowed to touch the cards, but have to instruct their surrogate turners to turn over this one or turn over that one. Beginners feel like part of the group and, though they may not be fully ready to absorb the card activity, they are hearing and responding to *this* and *that*. They may even begin to sense that *this* is for near objects and *that* is for objects at a greater distance from the speaker. Some beginners may also act as counters at the end of a game, verifying the number of pairs held by each individual or team. They may also record scores of a series of games.

You can add additional steps for slightly more advanced students. For example, after they pick up a card, they can read it aloud. A further challenge for advanced students is to require that they use their pairs in a sentence before taking them off the playing field.

Other card games

Once you have experimented with Snap and Concentration, you may think of ways to adapt other card games from your childhood. Consider Go Fish, War, and Old Maid. Students may especially enjoy creating the Old Maid card—probably calling it something else in this day and age, when the original title might be considered politically incorrect.

BINGO GAMES AND VARIATIONS

Basic Bingo orientation

Teachers at many grade levels and many subject areas invent Bingo games, and students generally enjoy them. However, unless students new to the game have a little support understanding the rules, they may sit quietly with winning cards that they don't even know that they have. The following orientation to Bingo takes some preparation, but you can use it for the rest of your teaching career.

On an inexpensive shower liner, draw an approximation of a Bingo card, showing 30 squares (5 across and 6 down), each large enough for a student to stand on. Write the letters B I N G O across the first row of the grid, and write "free space" in the center. Fill in numbers 1-5 in random order in the squares under the B column, numbers randomly between 6–10 in the squares under the I column, etc.

Gather as many students as possible around the shower liner.

(to one student) Stand on the free space.
(to another) Take a card from the table.
Go to the square that the card says.

Continue asking additional students to select cards and stand on the appropriate squares. When you see that a winning pattern has been created, yell, "Bingo!" Give students the name of that pattern (e. g., *across, down, diagonal, four corners*).

After the first winning pattern occurs, continue the demonstration until all of the winning patterns that you plan to use are identified and understood.

Bingo variations

Bingo can be played at any level of language proficiency. Beginners can simply look at a picture and match the corresponding picture on their card. Beyond that, the variations are endless. Teacher- or student-made Bingo sets can be used to:

1. practice categories. The caller says *B Fruit* and students cover one fruit in the column.
2. match homonyms. The caller says *horse—an animal*, and students cover *hoarse* on their Bingo cards. To win, the student with Bingo

has to create an appropriate phrase or sentence that uses each homonym that they have covered.

3. learn geography. The caller says *G City*, and students cover one word in the G column that is a city—not a state or a country. Advanced students have to identify the correct state (or country) of the cities they have covered in order to win.

It would be interesting to know how many varieties of Bingo teachers and students have created over the years. It's fun and relatively easy to design your own Bingo cards. Gather a group of friends together on a Friday afternoon and brainstorm Bingo games, creating cards and calling cards that are relevant to what you are teaching.

SIMON SAYS

In Simon Says, one student is Simon and the others line up facing him about ten feet away. Simon gives commands. When he says "Simon says" before the command, the students must follow the command. When he gives the command without saying "Simon says" first, the students must not follow the command. Any student who starts to follow a command that did not have "Simon says" before it is out.

Simon will try to catch people by saying his commands faster and faster so the students get caught up in the actions and forget to listen for "Simon says."

The game can start with simple commands related to anything they are learning or have learned. For example:

Touch your eyes.
Touch your nose.
Count to three.
Jump three times.
Turn around two times.
Etc.

If you have worked with previous chapters in this book, the following commands (along with many others) will serve as good reinforcement, review, and assessment.

Lift the sofa.
Sweep the floor.
Pitch the ball to the batter.
Swing the bat.
Serve the tennis ball.
Dive in the pool.
Honk the horn.
Wave the stick over your head three times.

WORDS AND CATEGORIES

For this activity, determine a list of categories and words within each category that would be suitable for your students—one that will stretch them but that they can handle. Provide starter word lists for each category. Some are provided here, but you can also build your own.

Each student will need a good supply of 3 x 5 in. (8 x 13 cm) cards, though they may cut them in half if they wish. Each card will contain a single word. It will not indicate the category it comes from. (You may allow students to draw a picture on their cards if they think it will help them learn and remember the meaning of the word)

Begin by sharing the starter lists (either those provided here or others you create) with your students. Students should copy the words onto a separate card for each. As a class, come up with more words for each category, which students should also write on separate cards. Later on, students may add other words they find to their card pile and share them with the class.

You should post a list of the categories on newsprint, and students should copy the list on notebook paper and keep it.

Once students have established a healthy pile of cards (including all categories), there are many ways of working and playing with them.

Starter lists

Fruits	Vegetables	Drinks	Cars	Animals	Languages	Human Body	School
apple	spinach	lemonade	Ford	dog	English	arm	classroom
banana	peas	milk	Dodge	cat	Spanish	nose	playground
peach	beans	tea	Cadillac	tiger	Chinese	toenail	teacher
		water					chalkboard

SORTING

There are a variety of ways to sort.

Sorting by categories: Working in groups of 2-4, students should sort their cards by categories—all fruits in one pile, vegetables in another, etc. By working together, students will inevitably talk about the words and categories and learn from one another. If you're comfortable with competition, the groups can race. When they finish, each group should read its list for each category aloud so all can hear and check. For homework, students can individually mix up their cards and re-sort them into the proper categories.

Sorting by knowing or needing to know: Ask students to sort their cards into three different categories based on how well each of them knows the word: 1) know well, 2) sort of know, 3) need to learn. Again, in groups of 2–4, students take turns stating a word they "need to learn," and having others in the group who know it explain the word and indicate its category. When no one knows the word, the group can call for help from you.

Once students have established respectable card piles, mastered the notion of categories (more or less), and learned some of the words and categories, try playing some games that students may recognize.

Category answer–question quiz

Students may be familiar with the TV quiz show in which the host gives an answer and the contestants provide a question in response. (This activity will strengthen students' command of interrogative syntax as well as their vocabularies.)

Bring three students into the Arena and prop each up behind a student desk or chair. Either you or a fourth student can be the host.

The host has a complete, unsorted pile of cards with words from all the categories. He shuffles the deck, selects a card, and gives the word in an answer format. Example: "The category for apple."

As soon as a contestant thinks he knows the answer, he says "Beep!" The host calls on the first student to "beep." The student gives his response in the form of a question: "What is fruit?" Remember, if he doesn't say "What is…," the response is incorrect.

Play the game with one group for a while, then bring up another group.

5.2 Games for Larger Spaces

A good way to devise outdoor language learning games is to go outside and see what the students are actually playing. For older students, check with their physical education teachers as well. Orienteering is increasingly popular in physical education classes, and it offers students wonderful opportunities to learn as they move.

THE HUNGRY WOLF

Play this game outdoors and use it to teach vocabulary, categories, and spelling. More than one group can play at a time if your playground is big enough.

For preparation, you'll need categories with short lists of items in each. Each student should have a copy of the list they'll be using to play. For example:

Colors	Animals	Classroom Objects	Clothing	Numbers
red	lion	chalk	shirt	one
green	tiger	desk	pants	two
blue	dog	book	shoes	three
pink	cat	teacher	socks	four
lime	zebra	eraser	tie	five
gray	cow	flag	coat	six

Divide the students into groups of six or seven. One student in each group starts as the wolf. He's hungry. The others huddle and decide which category they will follow and which member of that category each of them will be.

The students then line up facing the wolf, who is about 30 feet (9 m) away. (Determine the best distance for your class by trial and error.) They tell the wolf which category they have chosen. The wolf looks at his list and shouts the name of one of the items in that category. For example, if the category is colors, the wolf might shout "Blue!" The student assigned blue must step forward and spell the color (b-l-u-e) before the wolf runs up and tags her (or else she becomes his dinner).

If the wolf tags her before she finishes spelling the word, she becomes the wolf for the next round. If she does not spell it correctly, she also becomes the wolf, just as though she'd been tagged. If she spells the word before the wolf tags her, she stays with the group, and the wolf remains the wolf. Students should repeat the process for a few more of the same category, then switch to a different category.

Students in the group who are neither the wolf nor the spelling student must listen to hear whether the speller spells her word correctly. They can refer to the lists you gave them.

Of course, you can substitute other categories and lists. Use this game for whatever vocabulary you're working on. Also, make whatever adjustments you need to keep the play balanced, such as moving the wolf further away or closer, using easier or harder words, etc.

CATEGORY CHAIRS

Line up about ten chairs in the Arena, alternately facing opposite directions, as in the game Musical Chairs. Bring up one more student than you have chairs (i.e., with 10 chairs, bring up 11 students). Students form a circle around the row of chairs.

You or a student caller should have two piles of cards in separate boxes, one for word cards and the other for category cards.

The caller takes a card at random from either of the boxes and reads it aloud. The students begin walking around the chairs. Then the caller takes a card at random from the other box and reads it aloud. He continues drawing and reading cards until he comes up with a word/category match. When he reads that card, the students scramble to sit down in a chair. The student who does not get into a chair is out. One chair is removed from the row, and the process repeats. Last student in is the winner!

5.3 Word Play

Especially in the early stages of language learning, students cannot be fully themselves in English, their new language. They can play with words in their first language, but rarely in English. The activities in this section offer small ways in which students can begin to appreciate language play in English. At the same time, they expand their comfort with English vocabulary and structures, and they will recognize and perhaps understand a bit of North American culture.

You've taught your students plenty of English, but they're not really ready for life in this land until they've mastered those two great pillars of culture, elephant jokes and knock-knock jokes.

Jokes can be difficult for non-native speakers to understand because they generally stretch words beyond their literal shape or meaning. The humor is based on such stretching—puns, homophonic pronunciations, allusions, etc. To understand the joke, the listener must first grasp the literal meaning, and then reinterpret it in the way it gets stretched, requiring a flexible responsiveness to language that seldom comes when simply learning words and definitions.

These games are stretching exercises that will improve flexibility.

ELEPHANT JOKES

Using the jokes from the following reproducible page, give half the students a question and the other half a corresponding answer. (If you have an odd number of students, you get to play.) Then subdivide each half into groups of four. Each group of four should have either all questions or all answers.

Direct the students in each group to share what they have— questions or answers—and give them five or six minutes to make sure everyone understands the vocabulary of each item on its literal level. They may help one another, use a dictionary, or ask you for any explanation they can't find on their own.

     0-7682-3072-1   *Ready, Set, Speak*

Then, each with his own question or answer, students get up out of their seats and find the one person in the room who has the question or answer that corresponds to their own. The activity will involve a lot of talking, a lot of buzzing, a lot of moving around, and a lot of language. When a pair matches up, they should hold up their hands in victory, like a prizefighter.

Even when all pairs have matched up, some may still not get the joke. Sit the students in a big circle around the room, with the pairs together. Starting with one pair and going around the room, each pair tells its joke to the class. The question student reads his question, and the answer student reads the answer. After each joke, encourage students in the group to explain it. What makes it funny? How is the language stretched, twisted, or packaged in such a way that produces the surprise answer and with it, the humor? Try to draw explanations from the students when you can, or provide explanations yourself when you must.

You can then play the game again, either with the same set of jokes or with a different set. Thirty jokes are provided on a reproducible page, which should be enough for two rounds in a class of thirty students. See the Resources list at the end of this chapter for additional sources.

KNOCK-KNOCK JOKES

A similar game can be played for knock-knock jokes, but this one of course involves more ritual.

First, train your students in the pattern of the knock-knock joke.
Speaker 1: Knock-knock.
Speaker 2: Who's there?
Speaker 1: (Gives a name, word, or whatever.)
Speaker 2: (Repeats the name, word, or whatever.) who?
Speaker 1: (Gives the full answer.)

Speaker 1 will always be a single person. Speaker 2 can be anyone who hears the question—an individual, a small group, or the whole class.

Use the jokes from the reproducible page to create two sets of cards (or slips of paper). On one set, include the words "Knock-knock," and the response to the question "Who's there?" Cards that say "Knock-knock" are the question cards, so a student holding one of them begins the joke. On the other set of cards provide the answers. Divide your class into two—half the students on one side and the other half on the other. Using one set of jokes, give question cards to the students on one side of the room (one to a person), and give the answer cards to students on the other side. Then do the same in reverse for a second set of the jokes—answers to the first half of students and questions to the second. Everyone will have an answer and a question, but all their corresponding answers and questions should be on the other side of the room.

As with the elephant jokes, assign students on each side of the room to groups of four, and ask each group to be sure that every member understands the literal meaning of the words. That will be easy for the questions. For the answers it will be more of a challenge, since that's where the literal meaning jumps out of its skin and the word comes to mean something else. At this point, it's OK if students don't quite get the whole idea. Reassure them that they are fine, and that this kind of wordplay is very tricky.

Then, for one of the sets of jokes only, send students around the room to find their opposite halves. Once they have matched up, have each pair present its joke to the whole class. The pair (or one of them) will say "knock-knock." The whole class should respond with "who's there?" And on to the end of the joke. Try to have students explain to one another how the language twists to make the joke. Help where you need to. Then proceed to the next pair and continue.

Finally, repeat the process with the second set of jokes.

To solidify understanding, students at the intermediate and advanced levels can prepare a third set of cards, in which they further explain the meaning of the joke. In the panther example, that third card would read:

Pants are what I wear.

What do you wear?

FURTHER IDEAS

For further ideas, you only need to think back to your growing up, your children, or neighbors. What are the little word tricks that drove people crazy?

Pete and Repeat went out in a boat.

Pete fell off.

Who was left?

  (answer) Repeat.

Pete and Repeat went out in a boat.

Pete fell off.

Who was left?

  Repeat.

And so on. It's a way to teach *repeat,* at least.

　　　　　　0-7682-3072-1　　*Ready, Set, Speak*

5.4 Songs and Chants

SONGS

Songs offer a way of bringing bodies, minds, ears, eyes, voices, fun, rhyme, rhythm, and pitch all together in the service of learning language. Here's an old standard. If you don't know the tune, there are renditions of it all over the Internet. Once your students have learned the song, you can sing it with variations in the action, such as pat your head, slap your knees, turn around, etc.

If You're Happy and You Know It

If you're happy and you know it,
Clap your hands. (Clap hands twice.)
If you're happy and you know it,
Clap your hands. (Clap hands twice.)
If you're happy and you know it,
Then your face will surely show it.
If you're happy and you know it,
Clap your hands. (Clap hands twice.)

If you're happy and you know it,
Stomp your feet (Stomp feet twice.)
If you're happy and you know it,
Stomp your feet. (Stomp feet twice.)
If you're happy and you know it,
Then your face will surely show it.
If you're happy and you know it,
Stomp your feet. (Stomp feet twice.)

If you're happy and you know it,
Shout "Hurray!" (Shout "Hurray!")
If you're happy and you know it,
Shout "Hurray!" (Shout "Hurray!")
If you're happy and you know it,
Then your face will surely show it.
If you're happy and you know it,
Shout "Hurray!" (Shout "Hurray!")

If you're happy and you know it,
Do all three. (Clap hands twice, stomp feet twice,
then shout "Hurray!")

If you're happy and you know it,
Do all three. (Clap hands twice, stomp feet twice,
then shout "Hurray!")
If you're happy and you know it,
Then your face will surely show it.
If you're happy and you know it,
Do all three. (Clap hands twice, stomp feet twice,
then shout "Hurray!")

Follow-up

In addition to parts of the body and actions vocabulary, the song
ingrains the *if...then* sentence pattern into the students. They come to
realize that the first part of the sentence (the *if* clause) sets a condition,
and the second part tells how to respond to that condition.

Build on this pattern (without the rhyme, rhythm, and song) and
connect it to other realms of student experience. For example,
If you're late for school, go to the office.
If you're sick, go to the nurse.
If you have your homework, hand it in.
If you know the answer, raise your hand.

Little Rabbit Foo-Foo

Here's another old favorite that may take you back to your own
childhood and your warm, fuzzy delight with language at play. Use it
to teach vocabulary and gestures. The moral of the story even lets you
get into puns and old sayings.

Divide the class in half so that half the students are on one side and
the other half on the other. You read the good fairy's spoken lines.
Have half the class sing and gesture the verses that tell what Little
Rabbit Foo-Foo does. The other half will sing and gesture those in
which the good fairy scolds him. (They should scold and wag their
fingers directly at the first half of the class.) Gestures are given for the
first two verses, but students should apply them to all the verses.

Little Rabbit Foo-Foo

Little Rabbit Foo-Foo, (Hold up two fingers.)
Hopping through the forest, (Bounce your hand up and down.)
Scooping up the field mice, (Make a scooping motion with hand.)
And bopping them on the head. (Slap top of fist with palm.)

(spoken) Then down came the good fairy, and she said:

Little Rabbit Foo-Foo, (Wag forefinger no-no.)
I don't wanna see you (Wag forefinger no-no.)
Scooping up the field mice, (scooping motion with hand)
And bopping them on the head. (Slap top of fist with palm.)

(spoken) I'll give you 3 chances, and if you don't behave, I'll turn you
into a goon!

Little Rabbit Foo-Foo,
Hopping through the forest,
Scooping up the field mice,
And bopping them on the head.

(spoken) Then down came the good fairy again, and she said:

Little Rabbit Foo-Foo,
I don't wanna see you
Scooping up the field mice,
And bopping them on the head.

(spoken) I'll give you 2 chances, and if you don't behave, I'll turn you
into a goon!

Little Rabbit Foo-Foo,
Hopping through the forest,
Scooping up the field mice,
And bopping them on the head.

(spoken) Then down came the good fairy again, and she said:

Little Rabbit Foo-Foo,
I don't wanna see you
Scooping up the field mice,
And bopping them on the head.

(spoken) I'll give you 1 more chance, and if you don't behave, I'll turn you into a goon!

Little Rabbit Foo-Foo,
Hopping through the forest,
Scooping up the field mice,
And bopping them on the head.

(spoken) Again the good fairy came down and said:

Little Rabbit Foo-Foo,
 I don't wanna see you
Scooping up the field mice,
And bopping them on the head.

(spoken) Poof! You're a goon!

(Spoken) And the moral of the story is,
Hare today, goon tomorrow!

Follow-up

Review and check for understanding of the following words: *rabbit, field mice, forest, hopping, scooping, bopping, bounce, wag, slap, fist, palm, hand, hare, goon, today,* and *tomorrow.*

Bring a few students to the front of the room, and ask them to demonstrate actions as you direct: *hop, scoop, bop, bounce, wag,* and *slap.*

Share the expression "here today, gone tomorrow" with your students and give examples. Then explain how a little shift in the sounds of the words can make a joke.

Singing with gestures

The next song—also from your carefree days around the campfire— applies the cloze technique, whereby students progressively substitute gestures for words in each successive verse.

John Brown's Baby

John Brown's baby had a cold upon his chest,
John Brown's baby had a cold upon his chest,
John Brown's baby had a cold upon his chest,
And they rubbed it with camphorated oil.
Verse 2: Omit word *baby* throughout and do motion.
Verse 3: Omit *baby* and *cold* and do motions.

Verse 4: Omit *baby, cold,* and *chest* and do motions.

Verse 5: Omit *baby, cold, chest,* and *rubbed* and do motions.

Verse 6: Omit *baby, cold, chest, rubbed,* and *camphorated oil* and do motions.

Motions (not done on Verse 1)

baby	Rock baby in arms.
cold	Sneeze.
chest	Slap chest.
rubbed	Rub chest.
camphorated oil	Hold nose and make a face.

Follow-up

Review and confirm student understanding of the vocabulary: *baby, cold, chest, rubbed,* and *camphorated oil.* You may want to bring in some camphorated oil and give them a whiff so that they understand why they hold their nose and make a face. What other stinky things can they name or describe, and what new names can they learn?

You could also use the song as a pattern for conveying other vocabulary and gestures. (John Brown's puppy had a bone between its teeth… so he chewed and he chewed and he chewed. For *puppy,* students could bark; for *bone* they could stick a finger crosswise in their mouths; for *teeth* they could bare their teeth; and then of course, they could chew and chew and chew.)

And for students who must do cloze-type exercises in other classes, consider reproducing the song with the gestured words eliminated. Unlike many cloze exercises, this one will be understandable.

Bones!

Next comes a familiar song that will rock your students' socks, teach them language, and prepare them for medical school. It's also a good one to teach around Halloween time. If you can locate one of those cardboard Halloween skeletons, put it up on the wall and label its parts using the terms from the song.

Prepare students for this song by going over the skeletal parts. They say each part aloud after you and should touch it on their own bodies as they say it. Probably they will need a couple of run-throughs. Also, let them know that sometimes words are spelled the way people pronounce them: *gonna* for *going to,* and *whatcha* for *what do you.*

If your students know enough grammar to notice that sentences like *The toe bone connected to the foot bone* are missing an *is,* or that *them bones* should really be *those bones,* give them a gold star and tell them that songs sometimes do such things.

Once the students are prepared, get them all up on their feet and in the Arena, with plenty of room to dance around. As they sing the song, tell them to touch the bone referred to as practiced. The song should start quietly and grow in volume until you reach the headbone, then decrescendo as you descend. During the refrain in which the bones "walk around," tell students to dance around and wobble their arms and legs and necks as though there were no muscles holding them together. If you can borrow some drumsticks, claves, maracas, or tambourines from your friendly local music teacher, or even bring in some tin cans with stones in them from home, pass these out to the students and turn them loose when the "walk around" verse comes. It's party time in the graveyard!

Dry Bones
Whatcha got inside? I got… dry bones!
Whatcha got inside? I got… dry bones!
Whatcha got inside? I got… dry bones!
Clink! Bonk! Rattle-rattle! Boing!

Now connect them bones, them… dry bones,
Connect them bones, them… dry bones,
Connect them bones, them… dry bones,
Clink! Bonk! Rattle-rattle! Boing!

The toe bone connected to the foot bone,
The foot bone connected to the ankle bone,
(Tune begins going up by half tones.)
The ankle bone connected to the leg bone,
The leg bone connected to the knee bone,
The knee bone connected to the thigh bone,
The thigh bone connected to the hip bone,
The hip bone connected to the backbone,
The backbone connected to the shoulder bone,
The shoulder bone connected to the neck bone,
The neck bone connected to the head bone,
Clink! Bonk! Rattle-rattle! Boing!

Them bones, them bones gonna… walk around!
Them bones, them bones, gonna… walk around!
Them bones, them bones, gonna… walk around!
Clink! Bonk! Rattle-rattle! Boing!

Disconnect them bones, them… dry bones!
Disconnect them bones, them… dry bones!
Disconnect them bones, them… dry bones!
Clink! Bonk! Rattle-rattle! Boing!

The head bone connected from the neck bone,
(Tune begins going down by half tones.)
The neck bone connected from the shoulder bone,
The shoulder bone connected from the backbone,
The backbone connected from the hip bone,
The hip bone connected from the thigh bone,
The thigh bone connected from the knee bone,
The knee bone connected from the leg bone,
The leg bone connected from the ankle bone,
The ankle bone connected from the foot bone,
The foot bone connected from the toe bone,
Clink! Bonk! Rattle-rattle! Boing!

Clink! Bonk! Rattle-rattle! Rattle-rattle! Boing!

Follow-up

First, everybody crawl back into your coffins and take a nap. After that, review the names of the bones by pointing to your own and having the students say the name, or say the names and have students point. See if they can do it without referring to your cardboard skeleton. You could also teach *higher* and *lower*, *above* and *below*, and on *top of* and *under*.

Chants

At a certain age, some students are no longer willing to sing as enthusiastically as you might wish. Another way to wrap language around students so that it gets inside them is to have them convert any of the above songs to rhythmic chants.

In addition to such readjusted songs, here are a few chants to enjoy and on which to build some learning experiences. These do not require a tune, but they do need a good strong beat.

Weather chant

Mister Weatherman, please say
What will it be like today?
Yesterday the rain fell hard
And muddied up the whole school yard.
Today I hope that none will fall

So we can all play basketball.
Will the clouds all go away?
Will the sky be blue or gray?
Will the sun come out and shine
On all my friends and me, this time?
Mister Weatherman, please say
What will it be like today?

Follow-up

You can use this to begin teaching weather terms. What other weather terms have they heard or do they want to learn? Students may be able to create their own similar chant set in wintertime, when snow rather than rain gets in the way of fun.

Impossible chant

Students will enjoy the illogic of the next chant, and at some level they will begin to realize how language can distort as well as convey reality.

For this chant, a couple of students come into the Arena (the designated class performance area, see Chapter 3 and carry out the actions the chant describes.

One Dark Night In The Middle Of The Day
One Dark Night In The Middle Of The Day
Charlie's goldfish ran away.
Charlie closed his eyes to look
In the sky below the brook.
Charlie shouted silently,
"Go away, fish! Come back to me!"
The fish replied, "Oh well, okay.
My legs are tired anyway!"

Follow-up

What's wrong with this picture? Ask students to identify all the items in this chant that don't make sense. Some students may want to try illustrating the chant.

Adapting chants

After you and your students start using chants in the classroom, you find them everywhere. School sports chants are a good place to start. This chant comes from a high school basketball game.
One cent,
Two cents,

Three cents,
A dollar.
All for Pittsford,
Stand up and holler!

Not all chants have deep meaning, but perhaps you could create meaning as you introduce it to your class. With five pennies and a dollar on hand, say:

(holding up one penny) Who wants this penny?
Raise your hand if you do. (Someone does.)
Stand up.
Come here.
Take the penny.
Go back to your chair.
Sit down.
(holding up two pennies) Who wants two pennies?

Continue the same procedure until the one penny, two pennies, three pennies and the dollar are distributed. Briefly mention and write on the board that one penny is the same as one cent.

Who has the dollar? Hold your dollar in your right hand.
Raise your right hand high!

Continue asking "Who has…" with the three other students. Now they should be ready to act out the beginning of the chant.

When I say one cent, hold your penny in your right hand and raise your right hand high. Ready?
One cent! (The student responds.)
Two cents! (The student responds.)
Three cents! (The student responds.)
A dollar! (The student responds.)

Repeat this sequence until you can say it quickly and the students are waving their arms around madly. By now, the rest of the class—and maybe the four students themselves—are chanting along with you. Demonstrate one new word, *holler*, and you are ready.
One cent,
Two cents,
Three cents,
A dollar.
Anyone with money,
Stand up and holler!

The original four students can give their money to others, and this chant will continue longer than you probably wish it would.

You can vary the chant even further. If you'd like to check to see if students are prepared for class, try something like this.

Put your pen (or pencil) on your desk.

Put your book on your desk.

Put your homework on your desk.

Put a piece of paper on your desk.

One cent, two cents, three cents, a dollar. If you have a pen, stand up and holler!

One cent, two cents, three cents, a dollar. If you have your homework, stand up and holler!

Probably without even being directed to do so, your students will be waving their pens, their homework, or whatever else around in their right hands as they stand.

Other variations:

Practice colors (Anyone wearing navy, stand up and holler.)

Change the response from right hand to left hand.

Change the whole rhyme:

Textbook, pencil, notebook, and a file

Everyone who's ready, stand up and smile!

or

Sneakers, gym shorts, ball, and a sweater

I'm going outside to learn to play better.

Language elements

Questions	
What is...	5.1
Who's there?	5.3
If...then sentences	5.4
Homophones	5.3
Numbers (cardinal)	5.1, 5.2
Adjectives (colors)	5.2
Vocabulary	
foods	5.2
parts of the body	5.1, 5.4
school words	5.1, 5.2, 5.4
animals	5.1, 5.2
weather	5.4
currency	5.4

Resources

PRINT RESOURCES

Graham, Carolyn. *Jazz Chants*. New York (NY): Oxford University Press,
1978.
This was the first of many chant books published by Carolyn Graham.

INTERNET RESOURCES

For elephant jokes:
http://www.azkidsnet.com/elephant.htm
For knock-knock jokes:
http://www.azkidsnet.com/JSknockjoke.htm
http://www.lofthouse.com/humor/knockknock/
for songs and lyrics:
http://www.kididdles.com/mouseum/i007.html
http://www.niehs.nih.gov/kids/lyrics/happyand.htm
http://www.songsforteaching.com/

Name: _____   Date: _____

1. THE LIVING ROOM

window

sofa

door

television set

floor plant

floor lamp

easy chair

end tables

table lamp

coffee table

rug

serving tray

glasses

Name: _____   Date: _____

2. THE DEPARTMENT STORE

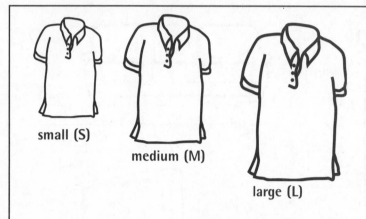

small (S)

medium (M)

large (L)

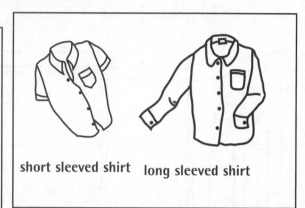

short sleeved shirt   long sleeved shirt

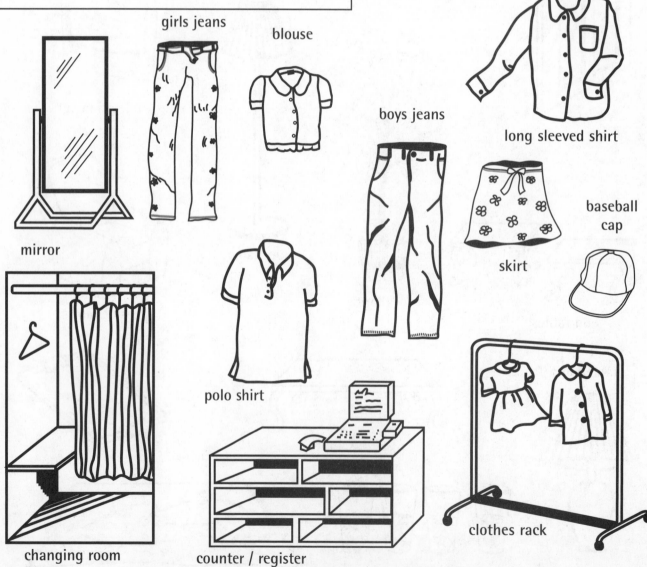

girls jeans

blouse

long sleeved shirt

boys jeans

mirror

skirt

baseball cap

polo shirt

clothes rack

changing room

counter / register

Name: _____ Date: _____

3. SPORTS ON TV

soccer ball

baseball glove

baseball

baseball bat

television

basketball

backboard

goal net

remote

swim suit

basketball court

SCORE 12 16

tennis ball

swimming pool

tennis racquet

tennis court

Name: _____   Date: _____

4. THE NEIGHBORHOOD

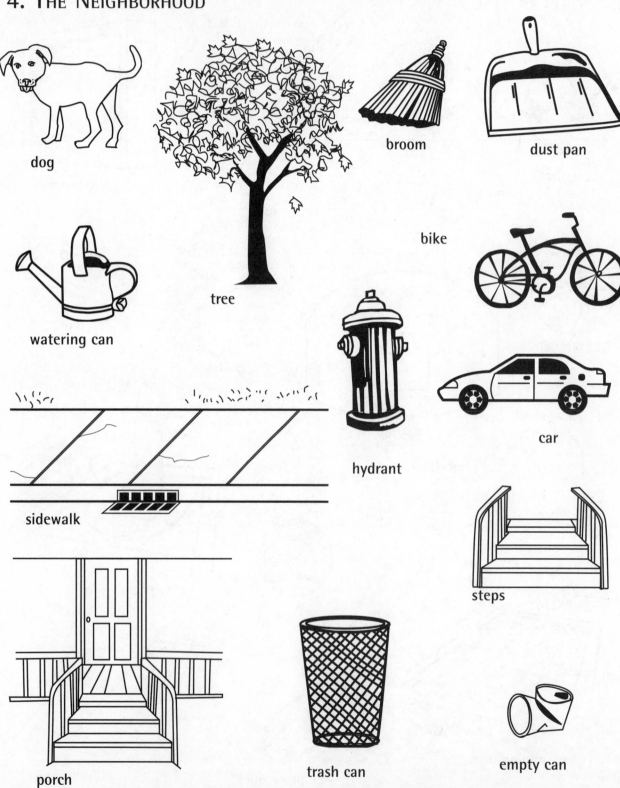

dog

tree

broom

dust pan

watering can

bike

hydrant

car

sidewalk

steps

porch

trash can

empty can

Name: _____ Date: _____

5. CINDERELLA PANTOMIME

broom

mean

joyful

sweep

mirror

smile

happy

ugly

laugh

wand

excited

beautiful

gentle

gown

sad

cry

frown

fireplace

angry

selfish

Name: _____   **Date:** _____

6. BILLY BEG AND HIS BULL

Cast

- Narrator
- King
- First Queen
- Second Queen
- Billy Beg
- His Bull
- 3 more bulls
- An old gentleman
- Giant 1 (He has two heads. Two students link arms for this part and speak the lines in unison.)
- Giant 2 (He has six heads. Six students linked together? Probably not, so try at least for three, and let the other three be imaginary.)
- Giant 3 (He has twelve heads! Probably four linked students is about as far as you'd better go.)
- The champion
- The princess
- The dragon (More heads than all the giants. Use one actor; let imaginations see the other heads.)
- Miscellaneous crowd (These can be the seated students who also double as the audience.)

Props

2 cardboard crowns

1 pointer or yardstick, which can serve both as a stick and a sword

4 pairs of cardboard or paper horns that will stay on their heads

1 medieval cone-shaped hat with a tassel

Part 1

Narrator: Once upon a time, there was a king and queen, and they had one son whose name was Billy Beg. (*Billy comes forward and bows.*)

Narrator: Billy had a bull he loved very much, and the bull loved Billy. (*Bull comes up next to Billy.*)

Narrator: The queen got sick, but before she died, she told the king that come what might, come what may, he must keep Billy and the bull together. (*Billy and Bull put arms on each other's shoulders.*)

Narrator: The king promised that come what might, come what may, he would do that. Then the queen died and was buried. The king married again, but the new queen did not like Billy and she did not like the bull. (*Exit Billy and Bull. Enter new queen and king.*)

Queen:	I cannot stand Billy's bull. You must get rid of it.
King:	No, my dear. I promised that come what might, come what may, I will keep Billy and his bull together. I cannot send the bull away. (*Exit king.*)
Narrator:	The queen was angry and decided to pretend she was sick. So she went to bed. When the king heard his queen was sick, he went to her bedside. (*Queen lies down on two desks in front of room. Enter king.*)
King:	What is wrong, my queen?
Queen:	I am sick, my husband.
King:	How can I help you get well?
Queen:	I am sick with worry about that bull. Only one thing will cure me, husband. You must get rid of the bull.
King:	No, my dear. I promised that come what might, come what may, I will keep Billy and his bull together.
Narrator:	The king went away, feeling very sad. But the queen stayed in bed and got worse. The next day, she asked again that the bull be sent away. The queen got sicker, and on the third day, the king returned to her bedside. (*Enter king.*)
Queen:	I am dying, my husband.
Narrator:	So the king finally decided the bull must leave. The queen was so happy that she climbed out of bed and went to see for herself.
	(*Enter Billy Beg and his bull.*)
Bull:	Why are you so sad, Billy?
Billy:	I'm sad because you will be gone.
Bull:	Don't worry about me.
Narrator:	As the bull was led out he spoke to Billy.
Bull:	Jump on my back, Billy, my boy. We'll see how well you can ride! (*Billy and the bull gallop throughout the arena as the narrator reads the following passage.*)
Narrator:	So Billy jumped on his bull's back and the bull leaped nine miles high and nine miles wide, and came down with Billy sticking between his horns. And then they galloped off to where you wouldn't know day by night or night by day, over high hills and low hills, far, far away. At last, they stopped.

Part 2

| Bull: | Now Billy, my boy. There's a mighty great bull in the forest here, and I must fight him. It will be a hard fight, but I will win. But first we must have dinner. Put your hand in my left ear and pull out the napkin you'll find there. Spread it on the ground, and it will be covered with food and drink fit for a king. |
| Narrator: | So Billy pulled the napkin from the bull's left ear, and spread it on the ground, and they ate and drank. When they finished, a great roar shook the forest, and out came the other bull. The two bulls fought. They knocked the soft ground into hard, and the hard ground into springs, and the springs into rocks, and the rocks into high hills. In the end, Billy Beg's bull won. Then Billy jumped on his bull's back and the bull leaped nine miles high and nine miles wide, and came down with Billy sticking between his |

	horns. And then they galloped off to where you wouldn't know day by night or night by day, over high hills and low hills, far, far away. At last, they stopped.
Bull:	Put your hand into my left ear, Billy, and take out the napkin. We must eat again, because I must fight another bull.
Narrator:	And again when they finished, a great roar shook the forest. Out came the bull, bigger than the first, and the two bulls fought. They knocked the soft ground into hard, and the hard ground into springs, and the springs into rocks, and the rocks into high hills. In the end, Billy Beg's bull won again. Again, Billy jumped on his bull's back. They rode away and then returned.
Bull:	Tomorrow, I must fight another bull. It is the brother of the other two. This time, the other bull will kill me. When I am dead, put your hand in my left ear and draw out the napkin. Then you will never be hungry. And put your hand in my right ear and draw out a stick. Wave it over your head three times and it will change into a sword and give you the strength of a thousand men besides your own. And when you have no more need of it, it will change back into a stick.
Narrator:	Billy Beg was sad to hear that his friend must die. But then he heard a more dreadful roar than he ever heard, and a tremendous bull rushed out of the forest. The two bulls fought all afternoon, but in the end, the other bull killed Billy Beg's bull. Billy Beg sat down and cried for three days and three nights. After that he was hungry, so he put his hand in the bull's left ear and pulled out the napkin, and he ate and drank. Then he put his hand in the bull's right ear and pulled out the stick that would change into a sword and give him the strength of a thousand men besides his own.

Part 3

Narrator:	After his bull was killed, Billy traveled for three days and three nights. He came to a fine place and knocked on the door. An old gentleman answered.
Billy:	Do you need a helper?
Gent:	I need a herd-boy to take my six cows, six horses, six donkeys, and six goats to pasture every morning and bring them back at night.
Billy:	What are the wages?
Gent:	Oh, it's no use to talk of them now. Three giants live in the wood by the pasture, and every day they drink up all the milk and eat the herd-boy. We'll talk about wages if you come back.
Narrator:	So Billy drove the six cows, six horses, six donkeys, and six goats to the pasture and sat down. At noon, a great roar shook the forest, and out rushed a giant with two heads, spitting fire out of both his mouths.
Giant 1:	Oh, my fine boy! You are too big for one swallow but too small for two! How shall I eat you?
Billy:	Any way you can.
Narrator:	Billy waved his stick in the air three times round his head. It changed into a sword and gave him the strength of a thousand men besides his own. Billy then lifted the giant up and threw him down, sinking him in the ground up to his armpits.

Narrator: That night after Billy drove the cows and goats home, they gave so much milk that all the dishes in the house were filled and the milk ran over and made a little brook in the yard.

Gent: That is strange. They never gave milk before. Did you see anything strange in the pasture?

Billy: Nothing worse than myself.

Narrator: And next morning, he drove the six cows, six horses, six donkeys, and six goats to the pasture. Just before noon, a terrifying roar shook the sky, and out of the forest came a giant with six heads.

Narrator: And again, Billy waved the stick around his head, changing it to a sword that gave him the strength of a thousand men besides his own. He lifted the giant up and threw him into the ground up to his shoulders.

Narrator: That night when Billy drove the six cows, six horses, six donkeys, and six goats home, the cows and goats gave so much milk that it ran out of the house, made a stream, and turned a mill wheel which had not been turned for seven years!

Gent: That is very strange. Did you see anything in the pasture, Billy?

Billy: Nothing worse than myself.

Narrator: The next morning, Billy drove the six cows, six horses, six donkeys, and six goats back to the pasture. At ten o'clock, a roar like a dozen bulls cracked the earth, and the brother of the two giants came out of the forest. He had twelve heads and twelve mouths, and he spit fire from every one of them.

Giant 3:   I'll have you for breakfast, my fine boy! How should I eat you?

Billy: We'll see. Come on.

Narrator: Again swinging his stick around his head, Billy lifted the giant and threw him into the ground up to all twelve of his necks. Then Billy drove the animals home. That night the milk overflowed the stream and made a lake nine miles long, nine miles wide, and nine miles deep, and fish swim in it to this day.

Gent: You're a fine boy, Billy. I'll give you wages.

Part 4

Narrator: One day, the old gentleman made an announcement to Billy.

Gent: Tomorrow, Billy, I will go to town.

Billy: What will happen there?

Gent: A champion must kill a fiery dragon, or the dragon will eat the king's daughter.

Narrator: After the old gentleman left, Billy watched many people passing on horses and on foot, in coaches and carriages and wheelbarrows—all going to see the great sight. After they passed, Billy dressed in the gentleman's best suit of clothes, got on the brown horse, and rode to the king's town. When he came there, he saw the grand arena and all the people sitting and watching. The champion walked proudly in the center, while three strong men carried his heavy sword. The princess sat up in the seats, looking very beautiful, but very nervous. Suddenly a great roar split the heavens, and the dragon came out. He had more heads than the biggest giant, and every one of them breathed blasts of fire. When the champion saw him, he turned and ran, and never stopped until he came to a deep well. He jumped in and hid up to his neck. When the princess saw her champion was gone, she wrung her hands.

Princess: Will no one save me now? Please, kind gentlemen, kill the dragon for me!

Narrator: But no one stepped up. The dragon smiled, and started to walk toward the princess. Just then Billy stepped from the crowd.

Billy: I'll fight the beast!

Narrator: He waved the stick in the air three times, changing it into a sword that gave him the strength of a thousand men besides his own. All the people watched as the dragon raged at Billy, and they fought a terrible fight, but in the end Billy threw the dragon and killed him. The people all shouted and said that this strange new champion must come to the king and marry the princess. But Billy climbed on his brown horse and started to ride away before anyone saw his face. As he passed the princess, she reached out and grabbed his foot, but he got away, leaving one shoe in her hand. Then Billy rode back to the gentleman's house.

Part 5

Narrator: A short time after Billy arrived back at the gentleman's house, the gentleman himself came home with a strange story.

Gent: Billy, it was amazing! The princess's champion ran away, and the dragon was about to eat her, when a strange new champion came out of the clouds and killed the dragon then rode away! No one knows who he was, but the princess pulled off his shoe, and now everyone must go to town and try it on to see whom it fits.

Narrator: The next day the old gentleman went to town and so did everyone else except Billy. He watched them go by on horses and on foot, in coaches and carriages and wheelbarrows—all going to try on the shoe. After they passed, Billy, wearing his raggedy clothes, walked to town. He watched as everyone tried on the shoe and tried to make it fit. Some stretched their toes to make their foot bigger, and others curled them up to make their foot smaller, but the shoe did not fit anyone. Finally, Billy came forward.

Billy: I will try on the shoe.

Narrator: The people all laughed and said that a raggedy boy like Billy could not be a champion. But then the princess spoke up.

Princess: I like his face. Let him try on the shoe.

Narrator: So Billy tried on the shoe, and it fit like his own skin. The crowd gasped. The king dressed him up in a velvet suit. Billy stood hand in hand with the princess, and they were married. The wedding lasted nine days, nine hours, nine minutes, nine half minutes, and nine quarter minutes, and they lived happily ever after.

Name: _____   Date: _____

7. ELEPHANT JOKES

What weighs 5,000 lbs. and wears glass slippers?

Cinderelephant.

If you see an elephant in your car, what time is it?

Time to get a new car

What should you do to a yellow elephant?

Try to teach it to be brave.

What should you do to a blue elephant?

Cheer it up.

What has 6 legs, 3 ears, 4 tusks, and 2 trunks?

An elephant with spare parts.

What should you do to a green elephant?

Wait until it gets ripe.

What is large and gray and goes around and around in circles?

An elephant stuck in a revolving door.

How do you stop an elephant from charging?

Take away its credit card.

Why did the elephant paint the bottom of his feet yellow?

So he could hide upside down in a bowl of custard.

What's the difference between eating an elephant and eating peanut butter?

An elephant doesn't stick to the roof of your mouth.

Why do elephants wear blue tennis shoes?

Because the white ones always get dirty.

How can you tell when an elephant has been in your refrigerator?

Look for tracks in the butter.

Why do elephants float in the river upside-down?

To keep their blue tennis shoes from getting wet.

How can you tell when an elephant is under your bed?

Your nose is squashed against the ceiling.

How do you get an elephant up an oak tree?

Tell it to sit on an acorn and wait 50 years.

Name: _____   Date: _____

8. KNOCK-KNOCK JOKES

Justin	Justin the neighborhood, and thought I'd say hello.	Wayne	Wayne, Wayne, go away. Come again some other day.
Fortification	Fortification, we're going to Miami.	Avenue	Avenue heard this joke before?
Water	Water you doing?	Dwayne	Dwayne the bathtub! I'm dwowning!
Toby	Toby or not to be.	Stan	Stan back! I think I'm going to sneeze!
Spell	W-H-O	Repeat	Okay. Who, who, who, who, who, who.
Tank	You're welcome!	Dewey	Dewey have to keep listening to these silly jokes?
Isabel	Isabel not working?	Omelet	Omelet smarter than I look.
Carl	Carl get you there faster than a bike.	Lettuce	Lettuce in! We're freezing!
Offer	Offer got my key. Let me in!	Harry	Harry up and answer the door!
I.D. Man	I.D. Man that you let me in!	Alison	Alison to you after you listen to me.
Anita	Anita ride to school.	Amanda	Amanda fix the refrigerator is here.
Juana	Juana come out and play?	Amos	A mosquito bit me!
Diploma	Diploma is here to fix the sink.	Atch	That's a bad sneeze you've got there.
Ida	Ida called first, but the phone's not working.	Charlotta	Charlotta bad jokes around here!
Yaw	Why are you so excited?	Saul	Saul there is; there ain't no more!